Government and the Environment

In today's global 'commercial society' an inquiry into the economic role of government is gaining momentum. Many crucial goods for the well-being of a society are not 'commercial': national security and clean air are good examples. This means that the economic role of government is not limited to cure so-called 'market failures' but it has to provide for non-commercial goods. Unfortunately in the last few decades the decline of the political-economic culture of Western post-industrial societies has left scope for people to blindly believe in a free, deregulated market.

This book brings the culture of the state in from the cold, by confronting readers at the start with the necessity of recognizing the fundamental difference between private commercial interests, whose provision rests on the culture of profit, and public shared interests, whose provision rests on the culture of the state. This book also explores how much individual well-being depends on both.

The only chance for public shared interests, with their non-profit nature, to successfully keep their ground in the face of the overwhelming power of private commercial/financial interests, lies in changing the currently dominant political-economic state culture. Governments and politicians in today's global 'commercial society' must understand their responsibility and social function lies in defending public shared interests, rather than in acting on behalf of private commercial/financial interests.

Laura Castellucci is a Full Professor of Economic Policy at the University of Rome Tor Vergata, Italy.

Routledge Explorations in Environmental Economics
Edited by Nick Hanley
University of Stirling, UK

Government and the Environment

The role of the modern state in the face of global challenges

Edited by
Laura Castellucci

Routledge
Taylor & Francis Group

LONDON AND NEW YORK

First published 2014
by Routledge
2 Park Square, Milton Park, Abingdon, Oxon OX14 4RN

and by Routledge
711 Third Avenue, New York, NY 10017

Routledge is an imprint of the Taylor & Francis Group, an informa business

British Library Cataloguing in Publication Data
A catalogue record for this book is available from the British Library

Library of Congress Cataloging in Publication Data
Government and the environment : the role of the modern state in the face of global challenges / edited by Laura Castellucci.
   pages   cm
Includes bibliographical references.
ISBN 978-0-415-63354-3 (hardback) – ISBN 978-0-203-09500-3
(ebook)   1. Environmental policy–Economic aspects.   I. Castellucci, Laura.
HC79.E5G668 2014
333.7–dc23
2013047920

ISBN: 978-0-415-63354-3 (hbk)
ISBN: 978-0-203-09500-3 (ebk)

Typeset in Times New Roman
by Out of House Publishing

Contents

Illustrations

Figures

Tables

Contributors

Simone Borghesi is Assistant Professor at the University of Siena and Co-Director of the Research Group R4S, Regulation for Sustainability. He received a Ph.D. in economics at the European University Institute (2001) and an M.Sc. in economics at University College London (1996). He worked at the International Monetary Fund, Washington (1998), at the Fondazione ENI Enrico Mattei, Milan (1999) and as Assistant Professor at the University of Pescara (2004–8). He has published the book *Global Sustainability* (with Alessandro Vercelli, Palgrave Macmillan, 2008) and articles in peer-reviewed international journals. In 2012 he was invited to the United Nations High-Level Meeting on 'Happiness and Wellbeing: Defining a New Economic Paradigm' and to the Fourth World Eco Summit (Columbus, Ohio). His main research areas are globalization and sustainable development, economic growth and well-being, European environmental policies, emissions trading, dynamic environmental models, and game theoretical models.

Annalisa Castelli is Assistant Professor of Public Economics at the Università di Cassino e del Lazio Meridionale where she teaches Public Economics and Environmental Economics. She obtained her Ph.D. in money and finance at the University of Rome Tor Vergata and has been visiting scholar at the Federal Reserve Bank of Atlanta. She has been consultant for the Italian Ministry of Finance, for the State Aid Department of the Italian Ministry of Industry and for the Italian National Statistical Institute ISTAT. Among her publications are: *Local vs National Environmental Spending: A Stochastic Frontier Analysis* (with S. Auci and D. Vignani); and *Inside the Blackbox: Economic Performance and Technology Adoption When Space and Product Relationships Matter* (with L. Becchetti). Her research interests are mainly focused on environmental economics, economics of corruption, and SMEs.

Laura Castellucci is a Full Professor of Economic Policy at the University of Rome Tor Vergata, and a member of the teaching Board of the Ph.D. Programme in Economics, Law and Institutions where she is responsible for the area Environmental Economics. Besides her intensive teaching and research activity, she has served as a consultant to various ministers (Transportation, Economic, Finance), to private firms, and as an expert in several commissions. She has been involved in various national and international research projects; at present she is involved in an Italian research project, funded by the Ministry of Education, as head of a Unit on Climate Change in the Mediterranean. Her topics of publication and interest include capital taxation, tax and incomes policy, underground economy, natural resources and technology, water use, energy, and the welfare state.

Berardino Cesi is Assistant Professor in Public Economics at the University of Rome Tor Vergata where he was awarded his Ph.D. in economics. He has been postdoctorate researcher at the University of Cergy Pontoise and Assistant Professor at the University College of Utrecht University (Roosevelt Academy). He has also been an economist at the research unit of the Italian Public Procurement Agency (Consip). His main research areas are public economics and industrial organization, in particular public procurement, economics of education, mergers, regulation, applied contract theory, and the economics of media. He has published articles in international peer-reviewed journals including the *BE Journal of Economic Analysis and Policy*, the *Manchester School*, and the *Bulletin of Economic Research*.

Manuela Coromaldi is Assistant Professor in Public Economics at the University of Rome Niccolò Cusano, Italy. She is a consultant at FAO. Her research activity is focused on public economics, microsimulation models, multidimensional poverty, agriculture economics, and agricultural policy analysis. She has attended several international conferences and workshops. She has published articles in international peer-reviewed journals such as *Social Indicators Research* and *Social Policy and Society*.

Alessio D'Amato is Assistant Professor (Ricercatore) in Public Economics at the Department of Economics and Finance, University of Rome Tor Vergata, Italy. He is a member of SEEDS (Sustainability, Environmental Economics and Dynamics Studies) and a research fellow at CEIS – Tor Vergata. He is also involved in international (CECILIA 2050) as well as Italian (PRIN) research projects. His research activity is focused on: theory of incentives, environmental regulation under asymmetric information, waste policy in the presence of illegal disposal and organized crime, and emissions trading. Several results of his research have been presented at international conferences and workshops. He is (co-)author of book chapters and papers published in peer-reviewed international journals, including *Energy Economics*, *Environmental Economics and Policy Studies*, *Journal of Environmental Planning and Management*, and *Journal of Regulatory Economics*.

Stefano Gorini is Full Professor of Public Finance at the School of Economics of the Università di Roma Tor Vergata and a member of the board of the Ph.D. programme in economics, law and institutions. He studied law at the State University of Milan and then mathematics and economics at the University of Oxford. Before being appointed to Tor Vergata he taught public finance at the Universities of Roma Sapienza, Cagliari and Sassari. His research has focused on the efficient provision of public goods, public debt sustainability, demand management in open economies, the economics of civil jurisdiction and social protection, corporatism and rent seeking, the role of ethics in economics. On these topics he has authored and co-authored several chapters and articles in peer-reviewed books and academic journals.

Amanda Spisto is postdoctorate researcher at the Joint Research Centre, Institute for Energy and Transport of the European Commission in Petten, The Netherlands. She has been postdoctorate researcher at the Department of Economics and Finance, University of Rome Tor Vergata, where she was awarded her Ph.D. in environmental economics and law. She has been also economist for Italian public authorities for energy and environment, such as the Ministry for the Environment, Italian Power Market Exchange, and the Italian Compensation Fund for Electricity and Gas. Her main research areas are: environmental economics and policy, economics and governance of natural resources, and energy system modelling. She has presented her research at international conferences and workshops and she is (co-)author of book chapters, manuscripts, and pre-review papers.

Mariangela Zoli is Assistant Professor at the University of Rome Tor Vergata, Department of Economics and Finance, where she lectures in Environmental Economics. Her main fields of expertise are sustainable transport and hydrogen technologies, environmental policy and organized crime, emissions trading taxation, optimal taxation and redistributive issues, individual pro-environmental behaviours, and sustainable consumption. She is member of SEEDS (Sustainability, Environmental Economics and Dynamics Studies) and Research Fellow at CEIS – Tor Vergata. Her research experiences include participation in Italian (PRIN) and European research projects (DIECOFIS, Development of a System of Indicators on Competitiveness and Fiscal Impact on Enterprise Performance). She is (co-)author of book chapters and papers published in peer-reviewed international journals, including *Ecological Economics, Energy Economics*, and *Journal of Environmental Planning and Management*.

Preface

Concern over the decline of the political-economic culture of Western post-industrial societies and over the unsustainable global exploitation of natural resources has led this group of economists to research and share their findings. The majority of the contributors are colleagues at the University of Rome Tor Vergata, differing in many respects, such as age, teaching experience, background studies and research specialization. In spite of such differences they found themselves speaking the same language in public and private conversations regarding, for example, the role of the state in today's economies, the necessity of paying more attention to the problems of the real economy as opposed to the financial one, the urgency of combating climate change, and the difficulties in providing for the optimal quantity of public goods and in curing externalities. Additionally, they found themselves sharing the same feeling that younger generations of students are ill-equipped to address such problems and concepts mainly because, being children of our time, they are lacking the very idea of public shared interests. Our effort has been to bring the culture of the state in from the cold by confronting readers with the necessity of taking into account the fundamental difference between private commercial financial interests, whose provision rests on the culture of profit, and public shared interests (public goods and externalities), whose provision rests on the culture of the state; and with how much individual well-being depends on both. In fact, to get the most out of this book, a careful reading of the first chapter is recommended as it discusses the foundations of such a shared vision, and explains the book's leitmotiv and composition. The first half is dedicated to general theoretical and policy issues and the second half highlights the wealth of contributions and guidance that sound economic analysis can offer to governments and policy makers facing particular problems in the area of environmental protection and resource use.

1 On the disappearance of the culture of the state from economics and the decline of the political-economic culture of the West

Laura Castellucci and Stefano Gorini

Outline

This chapter investigates the nature of the decline of the political-economic culture of the West, and the need to bring back the culture of the state into economics, using rigorous *economic* and *moral-philosophical* reasoning. It is a reflection on the *economic role of government*, in general and with special reference to the global environmental issues of the twenty-first century. The focus is not on the undisputed usefulness of designing mechanisms (institutions, governance systems, incentives) aimed at improving the working of the commercial and non-commercial areas of the economy, but on the recognition that *government enforced collective action* is the only – irreplaceable – social behaviour capable of protecting social welfare against the collective damage caused by the under-provision of global public goods and global negative externalities. The argument emphasizes the distinction and potential conflict between private commercial-financial interests, formally translated into the concept of rival private goods, whose pursuit rests on the *culture of profit and competition*,[1] and public collective (common) interests shared by the citizens of a political community, formally translated into the concept of non-rival public goods and externalities, whose pursuit rests on the *non-profit cooperative culture of the liberal state*. Today more than ever such shared public interests are primarily – though of course not exclusively – associated with three areas of the economic society: (i) all aspects of the real economy involved in the global process of environmental degradation and resource over-utilization, (ii) the dysfunctional area of global banking and financial markets, and (iii) the related trend of polarization in the distribution of wealth and economic power. In view of the inextricable interconnections between the real and financial fields of the economy, the necessity of government enforced collective action, which holds in the real field, extends to the financial one. With reference to Musgrave's classic distinction between the stabilization, allocation, and redistribution branches of public policy (1959), and to Stiglitz's essay on the economic role of the state (1989), this chapter focuses on issues not of instability and stabilization but of *allocation*. In particular, where reference is made to banking and financial markets the focus is not on their role in initiating economic crises, but on their failures in ensuring an efficient global allocation of capital between private commercial and public non-commercial interests (Friedman 2009).

Although this chapter's primary reference is the 'ground floor' occupied by economic society, its subject cannot be adequately investigated without going upstairs to the 'first floor' occupied by politics, and then further up to the 'second floor' occupied by moral philosophy. The chapter is organized around a sequence of concepts-propositions logically related to each other: (1) public collective interests, public goods and the non-profit cooperative culture of the liberal state, (2) the idea of a higher political-economic culture, (3) the intrinsic obstacles to the transition from individual to social rationality, (4) the role of public human capital or civic culture, (5) a behavioural code of secular social solidarity, and (6) the special spiritual strength of the belief in universal moral values. Needless to say, no critical rational discussion of concepts of this nature can ever attain the objective cogency of mathematical reasoning.

Public collective interests, public goods, and the non-profit cooperative culture of the liberal state. Contemporary liberal capitalist societies need to balance the market culture of profit and competition with the non-profit cooperative culture of the liberal state. Since the word 'state' has many meanings we need to sweep away any possible misunderstanding about what we mean by it in the present context. We do not mean actual government institutions, policy-makers and politicians, as such, but the individuals' awareness of the public collective interests they share with each other as equal members of a political community, and which form the connecting texture of an economic society that does not thrive only on trade and business. In other words, what we mean is – so to speak – a *core condition of the liberal mind*. Public collective interests are facts of social life, translated by economists into the abstract concept of *public goods* for the sake of theoretical economic reasoning. To better clarify our meaning we reiterate that in speaking here of public goods we are on a different wavelength from the conventional taxonomy based on different degrees of non-rivalry and/or non-excludability and on different types of groups/communities (Cornes and Sandler 1996). We mean only and precisely the public interests as defined above, conceived as the hallmark of a political community and as such by their very nature fully non-rival and non-excludable. The same holds for the meaning of *externalities*, but with qualifications to be explained later, because unlike public goods the latter are dependent on the commercial economy for their very existence, and thus are open – at least in principle – to the possibility of absorption (internalization) inside the market via changes in the price system.

The idea of a higher political-economic culture. Government institutions, policy-makers, and politicians are however the *visible hand* of the state in society, and in practice it is only to them that the sustainment of public collective interests in the face of the overwhelming power of private commercial-financial interests is entrusted. It follows that they must be bearers of a *higher political-economic culture* whereby they understand their responsibility and social function to consist not in acting on behalf of the latter and mediating between their conflicting pressures, nor simply in regulating and ensuring their contractual relationships, but in defending the former.

The intrinsic obstacles to the transition from individual to social rationality. The non-rival nature of public goods and externalities means that both the provision of the former and the prevention of the latter (when negative and not amenable to market internalization) are fundamentally dependent on *productive cooperation*, as opposed to competition. It follows that what stands in the way of the *transition from individual to social rationality* are not the supposed irrationality and/or bounded rationality of individuals, but the conditions hampering productive cooperation: (i) the intrinsic obstacles to voluntary cooperation due to the non-removable incentive to free ride on the provision of non-rival interests, (ii) the overwhelming strength of the incentive of individuals and groups to engage – through the exercise of economic and political rent power – in the distributional struggle endemic in the 'commercial society',[2] an incentive which is directly related to the growing polarization in the distribution of wealth and economic power, and (iii) the consolidation of ruling elites ever more unequal to the task of acting on behalf of the citizens' public interests (Judt 2010a).

The role of public human capital or civic culture. In order for this higher political-economic culture to find its way into the ruling and managerial elites bred in a liberal society, it needs to have roots in the social consciousness of ordinary people. It requires that ordinary people be sufficiently endowed with what Olson (1996) calls *public human capital* or *civic culture*, defined as a natural capacity to recognize the types of policies, rules, institutions, and incentives necessary for promoting and safeguarding their collective interests in the commercial society. A weak endowment of public human capital weakens a person's capacity to perceive the very existence of his or her shared collective interests, and causes severe distortions in that person's private and social behaviour.

A behavioural code of secular social solidarity. In order to be compatible with a liberal social order a civic culture needs to rest on a secular, non-transcendent, and non-ideological foundation, which we define as a behavioural code of *secular social solidarity*, or secular altruism. What is needed is a code of respect and care for the interests of our fellow human beings descending from the recognition that they have, in principle, the same value in society as our own, and identified by an essentially secular nature, in the sense that its imperative is not the principle of direct self-dedication to the neighbour's needs, however praiseworthy this may be at the individual level, nor the ill-defined and authoritarian-paternalistic principle of the 'common good', but the socially far more important and economically more costly principle of uncompromising honesty and sense of the state.

The special spiritual strength of the belief in universal moral values. This secular behavioural code competes in the minds and hearts of people against two powerful adversaries of a liberal social order, the *secular non-morality* of material greed, self-assertion, and power, and the *non-secular morality* of religions and ideologies, and if it remains without the support of an alternative non-religious and non-ideological but equally powerful morality, it will always find itself on the losing side. If it is to survive and succeed in exerting its invaluable social role for the preservation of a liberal social order, it needs to rise above the contingent world of the respect and care of human interests as such, to the *non-contingent world of universal moral values.* It needs to stand on the non-transcendent belief in the only public universal moral value compatible with a liberal social order, the secular value of individual moral freedom-independence as the absolute good in human life (see below, note 10).

Public wealth, the culture of the liberal state, and the need for a higher political-economic culture

It is a fact of economic society, known to public economics ever since its beginning, that in the commercial society of our day, half of social wealth is commercial, but the other half is non-commercial. In the conventional usage commercial wealth consists of private tradable goods, priced in the market, while public wealth consists of public non-tradable goods, not priced in the market. Commercial wealth generates profits, and thus profit and competition are the (legitimate) engine for its creation. Public wealth does not generate profits, at least not directly, so that the engine for its creation cannot be profit and competition, but only collective productive cooperation. Intuitive reasoning suggests that when a group-community is small the individual incentive to voluntarily cooperate, i.e. to share in the cost-effort for the provision of its shared collective interests, dominates the individual incentive to *free ride* on that provision. As the group-community becomes larger the incentive to cooperate shrinks and the incentive to free ride increases, until the former vanishes and only the latter remains (Olson 1965, 1988). It follows that in large political communities the satisfaction of common public interests requires government implemented and enforced collective action, under pain of complete commercialization of society, and social and environmental collapse. This insight, gained through intuition and non-formalized reasoning, can be converted into rigorous propositions using *game theoretic tools*. It can be shown not only that Nash equilibria entail under-provision of public goods relative to the efficient provision of Lindahl equilibria, but also that when the size of the group-community becomes very large the provision of public goods under free cooperation collapses to zero (see Chapter 2 of this book, on the failures of collective action).

Thus our chief proposition here is that, while there is no way in which shared public interests in large political communities can be sustained through market mechanisms and the related profit culture, there are also intrinsic non-removable obstacles to their pursuit through free voluntary cooperation. In order to be sustained they need a *substantial amount of collective enforced cooperation*, implemented by government through direct action and the design of appropriate policies, rules, institutions, and incentives. A corollary to this proposition is that if politically enforced cooperation is to efficiently serve its social purpose the mere fact of the political power of enforcement is clearly far from enough. The truly central point is that the culture that supports it must be the higher political-economic culture that we defined in the opening section as the *non-profit culture of the liberal state*. There is a wealth of 'technical' knowledge, from economics as well as from the other social and hard sciences, providing high-quality information for the design of government policies in any area of the economy, and particularly in the vital area of environmental protection and resource use (see Chapters 5–8 of this book, each offering an example of expert pro-environment advice on waste disposal, water conservation, technological lock-in, and forest governance). But if the ruling elites are not sustained by such higher political-economic culture, they cease to represent the state, becoming instead its negation; collective interests will be systemically displaced by commercial-financial ones, and the wealth of available 'technical' knowledge for their protection is wasted.

The need for substantial government enforced collective action for the protection of collective interests has always been disputed by social scientists and public opinion of conservative bent, particularly on the ground that an extended government increases rent, and stifles commercial wealth creation, innovation, and economic dynamism. Apart from the potential conflicts between commercial wealth creation and collective non-commercial interests, which are denied only by those who refuse to see them, our answer to this criticism is that the fault does not lie with government, but with the deficient and fast declining political-economic culture of the ruling elites, which are on a course of increasing identification with society's commercial-financial interests.[3]

Public goods and externalities

A large part of the economics literature dealing with public goods and externalities is implicitly flawed by a misconception: public goods are all too frequently conceived as one among the many cases of *market failures*, albeit an extreme one, and consequently the relationship between externalities and public goods is all too frequently viewed as one of degree instead of one of essence, with public goods being an extreme type of externality. But the fact is that public goods, unlike externalities, rent and market power, and informational asymmetries, are not market failures because they belong by nature to a non-market world. As already stated, we emphatically restrict the word to mean the stylized representation of shared public interests, which unlike rival interests cannot by definition form the object of market transactions, because if they did they would no longer be shared. This is more than an abstract point of logic. Since public goods are the negation of the market there is no way in which their provision can be implemented through profit-based market incentives. Their provision requires *productive cooperation* and the needed incentives are those encouraging collective productive cooperation.

Externalities are instead the true market failure *par excellence* (in consumption, production, common resource use, etc.). Though externalities and public goods are in essence different things, they are at the same time closely related. The essential difference is that since externalities are effects associated with market transactions, but borne by agents not participating in them, they are embedded in market transactions and need a market background on which to thrive. In other words, externalities are a structural endemic feature of the commercial economy. In contrast, public goods do not need a market background for their existence (and it is possible to envisage, at least in principle, a pure public goods economy with its own special efficiency properties). As for the kinship between the two, it is apparent by comparing the efficiency conditions of economies with and without externalities. The simple formalism of a market with externalities shows that the efficiency conditions are similar to those holding in the case of public goods: the marginal social benefit that must be equated to marginal cost is obtained by vertical summation of the individual benefits (negative when damages) borne by all agents (consumers or producers) affected by the particular activity (efficient total amount of activity), and each agent must face an individual price reflecting the effects of *his or her own* activity on those not participating in the transaction (efficient distribution among agents of the efficient total amount of activity). The point, conceptually important as it may be, has practical implications. There are only two ways in which a government can address the inefficiencies associated with the presence of externalities: either it is possible to devise rules and incentives capable of *internalizing* them, in which case the task of efficient wealth creation can still be entrusted to the competitive profit engine, or else the profit engine must be given up, or drastically supplemented, in favour of the cooperative engine of collective productive cooperation. Even assuming a competitive environment, a full internalization of externalities requires a radical change in the price system: from one reflecting only the benefits and costs directly accruing to the partners participating in a transaction to one reflecting all benefits and costs associated with it. This is a very tall order indeed for any price system! However, there are cases in which internalization is possible, and then it is worthwhile attempting it. But in most cases, particularly in the area of environmental protection and financial risk spreading, it is impossible, or possible only for certain aspects of the transactions. To the extent that significant externalities survive internalization mechanisms, any attempt to counteract them without breaking out of the profit principle is doomed to fail (see Chapters 3–4 of this book, dealing with the problem of how to counteract environmental externalities associated with large-scale accidents such as oil spills, and with the failures of policies to counteract climate change, respectively). Just as with public goods, the protection against environmental and financial global externalities is incompatible with a generalized global allocation of real and financial resources exclusively based on the principle of private profitability. Success or failure depends on the capacity of governments to counterbalance the competitive principle of private profitability with the cooperative principle of collective productive action, wherever this

is called for by the requirements of social efficiency in the global allocation of real and financial resources (Durand 2010).

Public human capital and the transition from individual to social rationality

The economists' approach to the study of *economics in government*,[4] the
complex interaction between government and the economy, has always
been, and always will be, subject to the strain of two opposite pulls. One
draws towards the question: 'What should governments do', the other
towards the questions: 'How do governments actually act? And why do
they act as they do?' In the professional literature and textbook conventions the dividing line between these two branches of economics in government, the normative and the positive, is relatively clear-cut, and both
are helpful in the support of public decision-making. However, the mere
fact of keeping them separate, useful as it may be for certain purposes,
reveals the congenital weakness of the idea of government on which the
separation is based. We believe that an effort should be made towards inte-
grating the two approaches into one, and we put forward such integration
as the *leitmotif* of this chapter. Our basic step consists in an upgrading of
Mancur Olson's concept of public human capital (1996), obtained by converting it into the essential ingredient of the kind of higher political-economic culture implicitly advocated by the late historian Tony Judt when
he denounces the persistent impoverishment of the political-economic
culture of Western post-industrial societies (Judt 2009, 2010a).

Contrary to the conventional wisdom of much current literature
which pretends to make irrationality and bounded rationality the main
culprits for the wasting of potential wealth – big bills left on the sidewalk – Olson believes (and we agree) that on the whole individuals are
fairly rational pursuers of their own interests, as they understand them,
but that 'individual rationality is very far indeed from being sufficient
for social rationality' (Olson 1996: 23). A similar view is expressed
by Benjamin Friedman in his critical comments on two much publi-
cized books on the latest financial crisis (2009).[5] Individual rationality
certainly allows individuals to pick up *some* of the bills that would
otherwise be left on the sidewalk, but picking up the really big ones,
by rising from individual to *social rationality*, requires efficient productive coordination among millions of individual and group agents.
There is overwhelming historical-empirical evidence that such efficient
productive coordination does 'not emerge automatically as a consequence of individual rationality' (Olson 1996: 6). It requires an enormous amount of *cooperative* effort that can only be brought about

by supplementing the competitive individual rational pursuit of rival interests with the cooperative collective rational pursuit of public non-rival interests. And this requires appropriate government policies, rules, institutions, and incentives. In their absence no effective obstacles can prevent rent-seeking from becoming the dominant behavioural mode of individuals, commercial-financial groups, government institutions, bureaucrats, and politicians. It is precisely such unrestrained exploit-ation of market and political power for rent acquisition in both the commercial and public economy, in disregard of public interests and negative externalities, that causes the great wasting of potential wealth described as 'Big bills left on the sidewalk'. Facing the question of why there is so much waste of potential wealth in so many countries and places, Olson suggests the need to distinguish between two types of human capital: a private marketable one, or 'personal culture', and a public non-marketable one, or 'civic culture'. He identifies the latter in the capacity of individuals and citizens to recognize 'good' policies, as well as 'good' rules, institutions, and incentives (which are in turn the result of good policies) concerning property rights, markets, 'impartial third-party enforcement', conflicts of interest, governance structures, independence and responsibility of bureaucrats and executives, and the like, and their related capacity to breed a ruling elite endowed with a corresponding political culture.

A self-feeding cycle of political decline

The concept of public, non-marketable human capital brings us back to the more general concept, proposed in the above section on public wealth, of a higher political-economic culture whereby governments, policy-makers, and politicians understand their responsibility and social function to consist in pursuing the satisfaction of non-rival public inter-ests, and not in acting on behalf of private commercial-financial ones and mediating between their conflicting pressures. As an economist, trained in the cultural paradigm of contemporary economics, Olson yields to the natural tendency of expressing his concept of public human capital in relatively narrow economistic terms. For our part, we believe that it should be given a deeper social and moral meaning, and to do so we carry it one step further by converting it into an ingredient of this higher political-economic culture. Our inspiration for such conversion is drawn from the latest writings of Tony Judt (2009, 2010a), in which he lays bare the progressive impoverishment of the political-economic culture of the West over the last 30–40 years. The *leitmotif* guiding his social-historical investigation is an 'ever-prescient defense of the role of the state in public life' (Homans 2012), which places him in the company of the greatest liberal thinkers of modern times. Using our conceptual framework developed so far, we resume and extend Judt's argument along three logical steps: a self-feeding cycle of political impoverishment, an 'open' culture of the state, and the social need for a secular public morality.

The impoverishment of the political-economic culture of Western societies and the related decline in the standard of their ruling elites over the last several decades, beginning with the Reagan–Thatcher years in the 1970s and 1980s, have evolved along two distinct paths, feeding each other in a circular way. The first has been the tendency to extend as much as possible the logic of the market into the non-commercial social domain, by subjecting traditional public sector areas to all sorts of institutional and normative market oriented innovations. This has caused – perhaps on occasions unintentionally – an objective contraction of the social space occupied by collective interests. The second has been the weakening of a culture of the state in the minds and feelings of people. The social space occupied by market principles and rules is by definition inspired by the culture of competition, profit, and commercial gain, whereas the social space occupied by collective interests is by definition not amenable to that culture. The objective displacement/contraction of the social space occupied by collective interests weakens in the minds of people the culture of the state underpinning that very space, diminishes their capacity to perceive the *very existence* of collective interests and breeds ruling and managerial elites without the civic-moral qualities required by the tasks falling on them in a civilized society. This causes in turn a further objective contraction of the public space, and a further descent of the ruling and managerial elites down a path of vanishing fundamental public coordinates and of vanishing capacity to perform their social function. And so forth.

An 'open' culture of the state

In introducing the concept of a higher political-economic culture of the state we felt the need to emphasize the obvious, that in that concept the word *state* does not refer to actual government institutions, but to a person's awareness of his belonging to a civic-political community, and of the interests shared, in his capacity as a member-citizen of that community, with his fellow-citizens. This raises the basic question: What do we mean, in the context, by a civic-political community? In a single word, we mean one that is *open*. A civic-political community is not an abstraction; it is a real thing in space and time. It therefore possesses all sorts of unique characteristics – history, culture, customs, values, religions, ideologies, institutions, laws, etc. – that distinguish it from others, and form its historically contingent *identity*. Moreover, since at any one point in time there are many different such societies/communities, generally speaking an individual belongs to one of them and not to the others. Now, to say that a society/community is open clearly does not mean that it must give up its identity, or be without one, which would in any case be practically impossible and conceptually meaningless (a political community without some sort of historical identity is unthinkable). What it means is that in principle any human being must be, and feel, allowed to belong to it irrespective of his or her own individual contingent characteristics. This in turn requires that a society's contingent historical identity must not constrain, via ethnic, racial, religious, ideological, political, social, or cultural barriers, its capacity of *universal inclusion*, precisely because the capacity to stand above such differences is an essential feature of its openness. We may therefore restate in a more intensive way the fundamental distinction between private and public interests, placed in the above section on public wealth as a cornerstone of this chapter. By public interests, to be distinguished from private interests, we mean the common interests shared by the members of a civic-political community, and identified by two strictly defining properties: (i) the political community must be, and be perceived by its members as, an open one in the sense of the just given definition, and (ii) the interests in question must be those that the individuals share in their capacity-status as members/citizens of that open political community, and perceive as such. It is these, and only these, shared interests that we refer to when we speak of public goods and externalities in this chapter. Formally, economists use the 'technical' concept of public good whenever there is a group of two or more people having a shared interest with the properties of non-rivalry and non-excludability. The results in the theory of collective action mentioned in the above section just referred to are derived using this purely formal representation, within which the special social nature of the shared common interest and of the group sharing it plays no role whatsoever. But as argued elsewhere (Gorini 2004), as soon as we probe beneath the abstraction of formal reasoning such special social nature does become important, and leads us to the following two conclusions.

First, in any society the individual agents of all sorts of aggregations and organizations may 'share' with each other certain 'group' interests, on the basis of their belonging to a common socio-*economic* status (occupational, professional, as holders of certain property rights, as users/consumers of certain services, as producers operating in the same area or type of activity, etc.), or of possessing a common socio-*cultural* status (ethnic, racial, religious, ideological, political, social, or cultural).

Though these may well have in many circumstances the formal properties of non-rivalry, they remain profoundly different from the common
general interests shared by people on the basis not of a common socio-
economic or socio-cultural status but of their being citizens/members
of a common political community. Even when they do have the formal
properties of non-rivalry, they can be treated as public goods only in
a socially very limited sense, because socially speaking their nature is
nonetheless more private than public. It is only the latter that can be
treated as public goods in the full sense of the word.

Second, even the common general interests of the latter type can be
fully treated as true public goods only when the political community of
reference is an open one in the previously specified sense. If its contingent historical identity is such as to constrain its capacity of inclusion
via ethnic, racial, religious, ideological, political, social, or cultural barriers, then the nature of the interests shared by its citizens/members is
ultimately more private than public. In other words, there is a strong
case, both logical and practical, for reserving the qualification of 'public' only to those interests-goods having not only the required formal
properties (non-rivalry and identification with a politically wide community), but also an essentially *secular* character, because *only a secular political identity possesses the capacity of universal inclusion*. Even
if there are obviously many public goods and externalities satisfying
the stated 'secularity' requirements, the ones associated with the global process of environmental degradation and resource over-utilization,
addressed in this book under the perspective of reasserting the vital role
of the culture of the state in economics, are particularly suited to the
purpose precisely under the secular perspective.

The relationship between a political community's historically contingent identity and its openness runs deep, and raises enormously complex problems, ideal and practical. An instance of the latter are the
current controversies and tensions within and among European nations,
in relation to the contrasting pressures for strengthening or loosening
the European process of political/economic/institutional integration,
on one side, and the worldwide migrations from less developed regions,
on the other. A more in-depth discussion of these problems is clearly
outside the scope of this chapter and of the whole book, but we want
to remind the reader that our remarks on the identity–openness issue
find again support in another of Judt's essays (2010b: Section XXIII,
'Edge People'). In explaining his estrangement from the currently popular national debates on 'identity', in the UK and elsewhere, he says that
although he was born and raised in England, and even shares some
of its prejudices and predilections, when he speaks of the English he

instinctively uses the third person, because he does not *identify* with them: 'What should they know of England, who only England know?' (Judt 2010b: 207). In an older essay (Judt 1996) he prophetically warns about the deeply entrenched obstacles to the progress of European integration after 1989, in spite of the common historical and cultural heritage and liberal social values shared by most European nations.

The behavioural code of secular social solidarity

The last stage in our conversion of Olson's concept of public human capital into an ingredient of a higher political-economic culture, takes us into the deep waters of *moral philosophy*. Here the basic question is: Can a higher political-economic culture such as the one outlined so far be sustained by remaining within the province of the narrow economistic perspective of private vs. public interests? Our answer is that it cannot, and we summarize its supporting reasoning by drawing on the philosophical analysis of the economics–ethics relationship developed at length elsewhere (Gorini 2009, 2012).

Interests are not moral values. As a basis for our argument we quote a proposition from the opposition speech to the Lateran Agreements delivered by Benedetto Croce (1929) in the Italian Senate in 1929. It expresses with classic brevity what we consider to be *the* fundamental theorem of moral philosophy: 'nearby or in front of the people who hold Paris to be well worth a mass, there are others for whom to attend or not attend a mass is worth infinitely more than Paris, because it is a matter of conscience. Woe to society, to human history, if men of such different sentiment, had failed them in the past or should fail them now.' We know no clearer, more compact statement of the three distinct but inseparable propositions forming the theorem: (i) the distinction between morality (universal values) and economics (contingent interests), (ii) the primacy of the former over the latter, embedded in the logically and existentially necessary subordination of the 'practical' pursuit of interests (the instrumental, the useful, Paris) to the 'moral' pursuit of universal values (the absolute, the good, a mass), and (iii) the great risks impending over the society where such primacy and indispensable subordination are removed from individual conscience.[6]

The comparative weakness of shared public interests and the role of a civic education-sentiment. The common interests shared by the citizens of a political community coexist with their individual and group interests in a condition of extreme comparative weakness because, as already argued at the beginning of this chapter, the incentives to act for the pursuit of the latter are strong, while those towards cooperation at community-wide level for the pursuit of the former are weak, sometimes non-existent, and much easier to be conveniently manipulated. But the comparative weakness of the citizens' common shared interests has also another cause. While both types of interests partake of the same nature, of being interests and not moral values, and of having therefore as such no moral status, they nevertheless harbour an important difference, not moral but social. Rival opposed interests divide people, while non-rival common ones bind them together. The former fragment society, while the latter form its connecting texture. And while a person's perception of his or her rival interests is anthropologically natural, his or her perception of the very existence, let alone of the importance, of the non-rival interests binding that person to the other citizens of the political community, is largely a matter of culture and civic education/sentiment. A person's perception of his or her rival interests needs no particular culture or civic education/sentiment, but the awareness of his or her non-rival citizen's interests does need them. If they are deficient, such awareness will be weak or absent. And to the extent that those interests are not adequately perceived, understood, and valued, even the best government and the most perfect system of incentives will never be capable of ensuring the cooperation needed for their satisfaction.

The secular principle of social solidarity. The other, possibly deeper, cause of the comparative weakness of public interests in relation to private ones takes us beyond 'culture' and 'civic' education/sentiment, into the province of morality. Let us start from the concept of social solidarity. Strictly, to have social solidarity means to have – in principle – the same respect and care for the interests of all other members of the human family that one has for one's own. The foundation of this behavioural code is the recognition that the interests of each member of the human family have – as a matter of principle – the same value in society as those of all others.[7] Thus social solidarity is conceptually the same as social altruism, where 'social' stands for the fact that the empathy must refer to every other human being *as such*. The qualification distinguishes *social* solidarity from the respect and care for people with whom a person has bonds of a personal nature, such as partner, family, friends, etc., which is no more than an extension of one's care for oneself (Buchanan, in Buchanan and Musgrave 1999). It also distinguishes it from the so-called 'group solidarity', restricted to people sharing certain characteristics (ethnic, social, cultural, etc.).

As far as a person's social responsibility and behaviour are concerned, social solidarity so defined has far-reaching implications. First, it implies an absolute commitment to personal honesty in social life. By this we mean much more than just strict law-abiding behaviour.

We mean an uncompromising behavioural consistency with the fact of regarding others' interests as having in society the same value as one's own. Second, it implies a sense of the state. By this we do not mean a vaguely understood civic sentiment, but the well-defined 'cultural' capacity of a person to recognize the common interests shared with other members of the political community, and to place them on the same level, or ahead, of his private interests. Third, it implies a disposition to participate in social redistribution. By this we mean the disposition of a person to contribute, in both his private and public capacity, to the interests-needs of other people *at the expense of one's own*. This third element offers the opportunity to explain what we mean when we define social solidarity as a *secular* principle. In the secular culture the commitment to personal honesty in social relations and the possession of a sense of the state are the highest social virtue, the highest expression of social altruism. In non-secular, ideological, or religious cultures, no special emphasis is placed on this eminently secular commitment, because the centre stage is reserved to commitments of a different type. One is the *giving to others*, the spending of one's own means and resources for the benefit of others, and more generally the direct self-dedication to the neighbour's needs, or, in other words, charity. Another is the social pursuit of something called the *common good*, an authoritarian-paternalistic concept overloaded with ideological-religious contents, proved by overwhelming historical evidence all too often to clash with the actual interests of individuals, or worse, to violate outright their physical and spiritual dignity. The deep 'cultural' difference between the secular concept of an individual's public interests and the non-secular authoritarian-paternalistic concept of the common good is a matter of fact. It is there independently of whether one adheres to one view or the other. Since those who adhere to the latter often fail to appreciate the difference, the only way to drive the point home, especially in their eyes, is to appeal to extreme cases, abundantly supplied by human history. Some of the greatest tragedies of the twentieth century were engineered by political leaders pursuing what they deemed to be the common good of their people, and perhaps of the whole of humanity.

As an attitude descending from social solidarity, self-dedication to the neighbour's needs, or charity, is undoubtedly praiseworthy. However, it is a corollary of our argument that living up to uncompromising honesty and a sense of the state is a socially and economically far more important virtue, and is generally more demanding. Consider the culture of profit in a world of no social solidarity (disregarding for simplicity criminal behaviour, on the understanding that the incompatibility between criminal behaviour and social solidarity needs no proof). Every individual would do whatever is in their power to do by legal means in order to maximize the satisfaction of their own interests, with no regard for the interests of others. This means, in particular, that whenever the conditions allow it, the individual will also seek to foster his or her own interests *at the expense* of the interests of others. In conventional economic terminology we say that a perfectly self-interested agent – the so-called *homo oeconomicus* – would not only act only in the pursuit of his own narrowly defined interests, with no consideration for those of others,[8] but would also exploit any available economic and/or political rent power in order to convert the losses of others into gains for himself. In a world of no social solidarity the incentive to bend markets and politics for the pursuit of rent-exploitation of everyone by everyone would simply be the dominant one. Now, the fundamental expression of social solidarity as we have defined it – absolute commitment to personal honesty and a sense of the state – does not in the least imply a denial of the culture of profit, but it does constrain it within severe boundaries that cannot be crossed. If one has, as a matter of principle, the same respect for the interests of everybody else that he has for his own, and values his common non-rival interests on a par with his private one's, then under no circumstances will he ever consciously exploit situations to gain advantage for himself by inflicting uncompensated damages on others (in technical language, to increase one's welfare not by creating wealth but by subtracting it from others). To make the point as clear as possible we mention three standard economic examples. (i) Consider the classic question: 'Should the seller of used cars tell customers the truth?' The question points to a typical situation of asymmetric information, found in many markets. Under our reasoning the answer is unambiguous: the commitment to personal honesty demands that the seller of used cars shall tell customers the truth. Any profit or other economic benefit obtained at the expense of others through their deception – however legal the withholding of information might be – is incompatible with the social imperative of personal honesty. (ii) Consider a firm causing negative externalities to other firms or people. Personal honesty demands that the managers subject their profit-seeking behaviour to the constraint of minimizing such externalities, or else of compensating for them. This – no more and no less – is in our view the proper meaning of the much debated, controversial, and often ambiguously defined concept of *corporate social responsibility*. (iii) Consider the other classic case, that of free riding on the provision of public goods (typically through tax evasion). Clearly, no free riding is allowed under the honesty and sense of the state commitment. In short, and more generally, secular social solidarity commands one to forgo any form of rent, and to constrain the competitive pursuit of profit in favour of productive cooperation, wherever the existence of public shared interests and non-internalizable externalities cause the profit engine to fail as a means of converting individual rationality into the social rationality of efficient productive coordination. We could say, using a general but perhaps too compact formula, that it prohibits the pursuit of any private benefit gained by causing uncompensated damage to others.

Obeying a behavioural code like this is a tall order, whose implementation in economic society may entail enormous private personal costs, especially in the form of the loss of potential profits and other private advantages that could otherwise be secured. Living up to absolute personal honesty and a sense of the state does not come free. For the individual agent it will always be costly, often enormously so, while for society it will always be enormously beneficial. The mind boggles at the thought of what would be the impact on economic society if absolute personal honesty and a sense of the state were understood and uncompromisingly practised by a sufficiently large number of people. It is an easy guess that most (though not all, of course) of the wastes, inequities, and evils of economic society would vanish. As a matter of fact, such understanding and practice are rare, and especially so among the rich and powerful, i.e. among those who are in a privileged position for exercising rent power. But this, far from relegating the code into the realm of a book of dreams, makes it all the more relevant in practice. The actual individual adherence to this secular behavioural code of social solidarity has a positive impact on economic society greater than any conceivable policy measure or business decision.

The liberal social need of a universal secular morality

We conclude the argument of the previous section with a rigorous excursus into *moral philosophy*, which, though abstract in nature, has great practical weight. It starts with four propositions, which we take as established moral-philosophical premises. (i) Interests, of any kind, belong by definition to the conditional, contingent, natural world of the useful, while morality belongs to the non-conditional, non-contingent world of values, of universal principles representing the ultimate good in human life, and thus also its absolute meaning.[9] Conceptually this is the only meaningful definition of morality. If we are not prepared to distinguish between the contingent and the absolute we cannot distinguish between the useful and the good, the boundary between interests and values vanishes, and interests, noble or mean as they may be, become the only standard of 'morality', i.e. the only standard of reference for guiding individual behaviour. (ii) Without the *belief* in some such ultimate good and absolute meaning of human life there can be no true morality. (iii) Morality and usefulness are a contradiction in terms: morality (the good) begins where interests (the useful) cease and vice versa. (iv) It belongs to the nature of these concepts that, at the level of individual conscience, morality must dominate over interests, or equivalently the 'practical' pursuit of interests must be subordinated and consistent with the 'moral' pursuit of universal values.

The concept of social solidarity introduced so far has been strictly defined in terms of interests, not of values. It is therefore a non-moral concept. In other words, the behavioural code of social solidarity, or social altruism, as defined so far, is strictly not a moral one. If the sentiment and practice of social solidarity are to acquire the power of a moral code, they must descend from the belief in something lying above the contingent world of interests, i.e. from the belief in universal moral values. More precisely, they must descend from the belief in a *secular morality*, embedded in the secular world-view, a morality based on the belief in individual moral freedom-independence as the unique secular value representing the ultimate good in human life.[10] We shall call it a *public*, or *civic*, morality because it is the only morality that can provide the moral foundation of the rules and government of a liberal social order without subverting it. In other words, the secular value of individual moral freedom-independence is the only value that can play a public moral role in a liberal, non-fundamentalist society.[11] It is then an obvious implication that if a person does believe in this unique secular value, his adherence to a behavioural code of social solidarity as defined so far will follow as a necessary consequence.

When we say that a behavioural code has not by itself the rank – so to speak – of a moral one, because in order to acquire that rank it needs to be supported by true moral beliefs, we do not mean to say that a person who does not believe in some concept of the non-contingent ultimate good cannot be honest, tolerant, socially altruistic, and behave in a socially responsible way. Of course he can, while the underlying motivations remain a matter of sentiment, natural disposition, or any other practical consideration of convenience or emotional well-being. What we intend to say is that, contrary to the view that it is only the actual behaviour of people that matters while the underlying motivations have no particular relevance, these have instead enormous practical importance. Reducing morality to a person's altruistic sentiments and behaviour, independently of what kind of awareness lies beneath them, is certainly a philosophical mistake, stemming from a deficient under-standing of morality's place in the spiritual life of human beings.[12] But it is a mistake going far beyond philosophy, into the midst of a social reality continuously subject to economic, political, and cultural strains. The distinction between social solidarity as a non-moral, interest-based concept, and the unique secular public morality from which it descends as a necessary consequence, is far more than a point of philosophy. The sentiment and practice of social solidarity descending from a belief in the universal value of individual moral freedom-independence as the ultimate good in human life has a strength and depth which, if it did not derive from that belief, it could never have. Although it is per-fectly possible for a person to possess an altruistic behavioural code even without belief in a concept of the ultimate good in human life, any sentiment of social solidarity that person may have, however deep and genuine, is bound to remain confined within the boundaries of human interests, whose non-moral nature is not converted into mor-ality by virtue of their nobility. As a consequence it can only be weak, not necessarily in terms of emotions and feelings, but in terms of its objective social and cultural status. If this secular social code remains without the unique support of some moral belief in universal values, then it is doomed to be displaced by the more powerful behavioural incentives carried into the social arena by the twin adversaries of a liberal social order and its secular moral foundation: the *non-secular morality* of religions and ideologies, and the *secular non-morality* of material greed for personal well-being, self-assertion, and power, pur-sued with all means as the primary motivation of life. If the sentiment and practice of social solidarity are not derived from the secular belief in individual moral freedom, but from religious or ideological values, they are perfectly capable of coexisting with a non-liberal social order, and with the actual violation of the moral freedom of the single human beings *as individuals*. Critical reasoning is enough to prove this conclu-sion, but even if it were not, there is overwhelming historical evidence to dispel surviving doubts (as we have already pointed out in warning against the non-secular concept of the 'common good'). On the other hand, if they are left floating over a morally empty background they will simply be too weak to succeed in preventing the trampling of indi-vidual and group interests over each other and over collectively shared public interests, and in preventing the pursuit of wealth-destructing rent-exploitation in the distributional struggle from becoming the dominant 'non-moral' behavioural code in society. The survival of a secular code of social solidarity as we have defined it, drawing on the economic, social, and moral insights of Olson and Judt, is a necessary condition for the preservation of a liberal social order, and for sustaining the collective action needed to defend today's global commercial society against its enormous environmental market failures. But if it is to survive and succeed in the social arena, this secular code needs the superior strength reclaimed with unequalled clarity by Croce: it must rise above the contingent world of respect and care for human interests *as such*, into the *non-contingent world of the secular universal value* of individual moral freedom-independence as the absolute good in human life.

Notes

1 We are using here the word 'competition' with a different meaning from that of 'competitive market conditions'. What we are referring to is a particular coordination modality of inter-agent economic activity, alternative to the cooperative mode. Thus the competitive coordination modality is perfectly compatible with any degree of rent power. Competition is, precisely and simply, the alternative to cooperation (Hall and Soskice 2001).
2 This highly suggestive terminology was made famous by Adam Smith, who used it to characterize the economic society of the early capitalism of his day, and whose subsequent global expansion he predicted.
3 A notable example is offered by the recent popular riots in Brazil. Until not long ago the country was advertised in the West as an emerging world model of economic progress. The bulk of ordinary people have reminded us that while the country has the worst health service and school system in the world its (progressive) government is channelling immense amounts of resources into the 2014 World Cup and 2016 Olympics.
4 This is the name used by the *Journal of Economic Perspectives* for some of its best-known invited lectures in the 1990s.
5 The books are George A. Akerlof and Robert J. Shiller, *Animal Spirits: How Human Psychology Drives the Economy, and Why It Matters for Global Capitalism* (Princeton: Princeton University Press, 2009) and Robert J. Shiller, *The Subprime Solution: How Today's Global Financial Crisis Happened, and What to Do About It* (Princeton: Princeton University Press, 2009).
6 'accanto o di fronte agli uomini che stimano Parigi valer bene una messa, sono altri pei quali l'ascoltare o no una messa è cosa che vale infinitamente più di Parigi, perché è affare di coscienza. Guai alla società, alla storia umana, se uomini che così diversamente sentono, le fossero mancati o le mancassero!' Needless to say, we are using here the word 'theorem' as a metaphor. Moral philosophy is not mathematics, and the logic of philosophy, though logic all the same, cannot be reduced to the logic of mathematics.
7 We will not go into the currently much researched topic of (non-human) animal morality.
8 Who in the classic language of Buchanan (in Buchanan and Musgrave 1999) are regarded only as part of the natural world.
9 It lies at the heart of the secular world-view that the concepts of absolute goodness and absolute meaning belong exclusively to the moral universe of statements about values, having no place whatsoever in the 'existential'

universe of statements about facts and reality. In non-secular views those concepts are instead brought back inside the 'existential' universe of metaphysical statements about the reality and goodness of the divine, or the absolute goodness or evil of certain facts and conditions of the social world, by means of a logical process that under the rules of critical rationalism is philosophically untenable.

10 Following Croce (1943) we distinguish freedom as a moral concept, which coincides with individual consciousness and self-consciousness, from freedom as a practical concept, which refers to individual freedom of action in society and belongs to the province of social theory, not of moral philosophy (Berlin 1969).

11 The reasoning in support of the moral-philosophical statements contained in this and the previous paragraphs is reduced here to a minimum in order not to overburden the chapter. It is exhaustively developed in Gorini (2009).

12 The study of moral behavior in humans and other animals as a fact of nature has long been under investigation by neuroscientists. Our position is not a criticism of their work, which appears to be making great scientific progress. It is that the morality of moral philosophy is a different thing from the morality of science. An example of the problems tackled by the neuroscientific approach can be found in Churchland (2006).

References

Berlin, I. 1969. *Four Essays on Liberty*. Oxford: Oxford University Press.

Buchanan, J. M. and Musgrave, R. A. 1999. *Public Finance and Public Choice: Two Contrasting Visions of the State*. Cambridge, MA: MIT Press.

Churchland, P. 2006. 'Do We Have Free Will?'. *New Scientist*, 18 November.

Cornes, R. and Sandler, T. 1996. *The Theory of Externalities, Public Goods, and Club Goods*, 2nd edition. Cambridge: Cambridge University Press.

Croce, B. 1929. Opposition speech to the Lateran Agreements, in the Italian Senate. Quoted from A. C. Jemolo, *Chiesa e Stato in Italia negli ultimi cento anni*, 3rd revised edition. Turin: Einaudi, 1971, p. 496.

Croce, B. 1943. 'Revisione filosofica dei concetti di "libertà" e "giustizia"'. *La Critica*, 41(5): 276–84. Reprinted in B. Croce and L. Einaudi, *Liberismo e liberalismo*, 2nd edition. Milan and Naples: Riccardo Ricciardi Editore, 1988, pp. 85–97.

Durand, D. 2010. 'Parigi e Berlino non sono una coppia'. *L'Euro senza Europa*, I quaderni speciali di *Limes*, April.

Friedman, B. 2009. 'The Failure of the Economy & the Economists'. *The New York Review of Books*, 28 May.

Gorini, S. 2004. 'Corporatismo', in *Enciclopedia del Novecento*, III Supplemento: *Dal XX al XXI secolo: problemi e prospettive*. Rome: Istituto dell'Enciclopedia Italiana, pp. 249–56.

Gorini, S. 2009. 'An Economist's *Plaidoyer* for a Secular Ethics: The Moral Foundation and Social Role of Critical Rationalism', in J. Brennan and G. Eusepi (eds.), *The Economics of Ethics and the Ethics of Economics: Values, Markets and the State*. Cheltenham: Edward Elgar, pp. 32–50.

Gorini, S. 2012. 'The Intellectual, Moral and Scientific Legacy of Sergio Steve in the Personal Revisitation by a Former Research Student'. *Rivista di Storia Economica*, 2: 351–65.

Hall, P. A. and Soskice, D. 2001. 'An Introduction to Varieties of Capitalism', in P. A. Hall and D. Soskice (eds.), *Varieties of Capitalism: The Institutional Foundations of Comparative Advantage*. Oxford: Oxford University Press, pp. 1–68.

Homans, J. A. 2012. 'Tony Judt: A Final Victory'. *The New York Review of Books*, 22 March. (Essay by Tony Judt's wife on his very last book, *Thinking the Twentieth Century*, written with Timothy Snyder).

Judt, T. 1996. *A Grand Illusion: An Essay on Europe*. New York: Hill & Wang.

Judt, T. 2009. 'What is Living and What is Dead in Social Democracy?'. *The New York Review of Books*, 17 December.

Judt, T. 2010a. *Ill Fares the Land: A Treatise on our Present Discontent*. London: Allen Lane.

Judt, T. 2010b. *The Memory Chalet*. London: Heinemann.

Musgrave, R. A. 1959. *The Theory of Public Finance*. New York: McGraw-Hill.

Olson, M. 1965. *The Logic of Collective Action: Public Goods and the Theory of Groups*. Cambridge, MA: Harvard University Press.

Olson, M. 1988. 'Collective Action', in J. Eatwell, M. Milgate and P. Newman (eds.), *The New Palgrave: A Dictionary of Economics*. Basingstoke: Palgrave Macmillan.

Olson, M. 1996. 'Big Bills Left on the Sidewalk: Why Some Nations are Rich, and Others Poor'. *Journal of Economic Perspectives*, 10(2): 3–24.

Stiglitz, J. E. et al. 1989. *The Economic Role of the State*. Oxford: Blackwell.

2 The failures of collective action

A formal game-theoretic revisitation of the Olson theory

Berardino Cesi and Stefano Gorini

Introduction

This chapter is an inquiry into the nature and causes of the failures of collective action. We draw our inspiration from the ideas developed by Mancur Olson in his major work (1965), and resumed in his essays (1988, 1996). But ours is a relatively simple analytical purpose. We consider a group-community of people (or more generally of *individual* agents) bound together by one or more common, shared interests, whose satisfaction requires some kind of collective action. We shall denote the collective action aimed at satisfying those common interests by G, which, under the usual conventional definitions, is to be interpreted as a given amount-quantity of group goods, non-rival and non-excludable among the group's members. Each member of the group derives an individual benefit from G. On the other hand, implementing the collective action G has a cost. For a member of the group, contributing to the collective action means bearing a share of its cost, while not contributing means free riding on G, because G is *by definition* non-rival and non-excludable. We focus our attention on the relationship between the individual incentive to contribute and the individual incentive to free ride under two distinct social states: (i) a social state of *free cooperation* and (ii) a social state of *enforced (or mandatory) cooperation* within a group endowed with an *organization*. By a group acting under free cooperation we mean one whose members are totally free and independent from each other in all their actions, so that if they share some common interest, implementing the collective action G depends entirely on a fully free, voluntary interaction–cooperation of each one with all the others. By an organized group acting under enforced cooperation we mean one endowed with a governance structure, i.e. by an internal system of power which enables the group to enforce rules and behaviours upon its members, specifically to make a member's contributing to the cost of *G* into a social obligation whose violation is socially sanctioned by a penalty. Drawing on game literature on cartel equilibria and repeated games (Abreu 1988; Abreu et al. 1986, 1994; Wen 1994), and using only simple standard concepts of pure strategies and Nash equilibria in static one-stage and dynamic repeated games we investigate the formal conditions, structural (individual benefits and costs) and behavioural (expected individual payoffs), under which the individual incentive to contribute to the collective action dominates over the individual incentive to free ride, or vice versa. The central premise underlying the formal investigation is that there are intrinsic non-removable obstacles to the implementing of collective actions for the pursuit of common shared interests under free cooperation. Insofar as a group-community stays in a social condition of pure free cooperation, such obstacles are non-removable because they are intrinsically embedded in the fact that the satisfaction of common shared interests is, by its very nature, open to the unrestraint possibility of free riding.

In short, under free cooperation the relative strength of the incentive to contribute over the incentive to free ride (which is a socially fully legitimate choice subject to no social sanction) depends essentially, on one hand on the probability of a member's free riding being perceived/detected by the others, which is in turn intrinsically dependent on the size of the group-community, and on the other on the importance that the members give to the future relative to the present. When the incentive to free ride dominates over the incentive to contribute the collective action collapses to zero. This may be the end of the story, but it might also not be, depending on the nature of the group and collective action in question. If the collective action in question is collectively perceived by the group's members as sufficiently important for their general welfare, then the fact that under free cooperation it would not be undertaken may be one of the reasons – though not necessarily the only or primary one – why the group itself evolves from a totally free aggregation into an organization.

Under enforced cooperation the relative strength of the incentive to contribute over the incentive to free ride (which becomes a socially sanctioned violation of a social obligation) depends essentially, on one hand on the excess of the expected penalty over the mandatory social obligation to contribute, and on the other – as before – on the importance that the members give to the future relative to the present. When the incentive to free ride dominates over the incentive to contribute the collective action does not collapse to zero because it is the responsibility of the group's organization to continue to implement it. But it is a sign that the organization is not functioning, and if it proves to be incapable of reversing the situation it is unlikely to survive.

In general, our formal analysis makes no reference to the particular kind of group-community, common shared interests, and collective action G under consideration. However, two distinctions are important for assessing its social relevance. The first distinction concerns the nature of the collective action. It may be a *wealth creating* activity, in which case G stands for actual group goods whose production increases the general wealth of society at large. But it may also be a *wealth destructing* activity, when it stands for the group's engagement in the distributional struggle between the group itself and the other groups and individuals of society at large, in other words for the group's engagement not in wealth creation but in rent acquisition. The second distinction concerns the nature of the group-community. The group may be a particular subset of agents in society, sharing some common interests belonging only to them, or it may be the *political-civic community* itself, in its entirety. It is only in the latter case that we define the common interests shared by the community's members – in their capacity as citizens – to be *public* interests, the collective action G aimed at their satisfaction as representing *public* goods, and the community's organization to coincide with the *political government* (an extensive explanation of these central concepts, going far beyond the limitations of mathematical formalism, is provided in Chapter 1 of the book). We want to make it clear that although our formal analysis is not affected by such interpretative distinctions, it is precisely the latter case that we have implicitly in mind in presenting and discussing its results.

In the next section on one-stage games we study the problem of whether group goods which are in fixed supply and subject to a fixed cost of production will be supplied or not supplied in a static one-stage game of free cooperation, showing how the final outcome depends on the size of the group. Next, in the section on repeated games of free cooperation, we carry the previous analysis into a dynamic repeated game of free cooperation, showing how the final outcome depends both on the size of the group and on the value given to the future by the group members. Next, in the section on repeated games of enforced cooperation, we study how the outcome of the previous section is affected when we move from a state of free cooperation to one of enforced cooperation under an organized group. Finally, in the last section we extend the analysis of the section on one-stage games to the case of group goods which are in variable supply and subject to a variable cost of production, showing how under a static one-stage game of free cooperation the supply of the goods is inefficiently low, and how this insufficiency increases to the point of complete collapse when the group becomes very large.

A one-stage game of free cooperation: the role of group size

Given a group-community as defined in the Introduction, let G be a given quantity-quality of group goods, non-rival and non-excludable among the group's members. In this model G is in fixed supply. It is either supplied or not supplied. The issue of the efficient level of G under a variable supply is postponed to the last section.

The group consists of a number N of representative members (agents). The individual benefit derived from the given G by each member of the group is normalized to G itself.

E is the total cost of producing G.

We consider a *static one-stage game SG* of free cooperation (as defined in the Introduction). Free cooperation within the group requires that its members spend time and effort interacting with each other in order to arrange their cooperation for implementing the collective action. This is a cost of free cooperation. Clearly the *total* (collective) amount of time and effort spent on arranging cooperation increases with the increase in group size. We shall take it as an acceptable first approximation that the *interaction cost per agent* is constant, and denote it by α. The level of α will in turn depend on the nature of the group and of the collective action under investigation, and of course also on the degree of cooperative spirit among the group's members (the more cooperatively minded are the members, the lower is α). Let $N \geq 2$ be the size of the group (a definitional condition because with $N = 1$ no question of collective action would arise in the first place). Each agent has a choice between two strategies: the strategy C of contributing to the collective action and the strategy F of not contributing (or free riding, deviating, defecting). We assume no differential cost sharing among the group's members. If M agents contribute and the remaining $N - M$ do not, all contributing agents bear the same cost, equal to the cost of G per contributing agent $E/M + \alpha$, with $M \leq N \geq 2$ (the no differential cost sharing assumption will be partially removed in the last section).

The equilibrium outcomes of the SG turn out to be relatively simple. Consider separately the two alternative states. In one the combination of G, E, α, N yields $G \leq E/N + \alpha$, in the other it yields $G > E/N + \alpha$.

Let $G \leq E/N + \alpha$. Even if all agents choose to contribute, the individual benefit derived from the collective action is less than, or at most equal to, its individual cost. Trivially, not contributing is the best choice for everyone, and the collective action is not undertaken.

Let $G > E/N + \alpha$. Here the situation is slightly more complex. Define the number $m \leq N$ by the following positive payoff condition

$$m = \min\{M \leq N \mid G > E/M + a\} \tag{1}$$

identifying the minimum size of a subgroup of contributing agents, required to ensure that their payoff from contributing be positive. If exactly m agents contribute, their individual payoff is

$$U_C = G - (E/m + \alpha) > 0 \qquad (2)$$

while the individual payoff of the $N - m$ agents who deviate is

$$U_F = G > U_C \qquad (3)$$

There are two possibilities, $m = 1$ and $1 < m \leq N$.

(i) The case $m = 1$ means $G > E + \alpha$. If a single agent still benefits from G even if he has to bear the whole cost, then, even when $N - 1$ agents defect, the best choice for him is to act unilaterally. On the other hand, if any single agent does act unilaterally, then the best choice for the remaining $N - 1$ agents is to defect. There are therefore N distinct Nash equilibria NE, one for each agent acting unilaterally and all the others $N - 1$ defecting.

(ii) The case $1 < m \leq N$ implies $G \leq E + \alpha$. In this case there is more than one type of NE. In fact there are two *coexisting* types of NE.

One type is the (unique) equilibrium where no one contributes. Since $G \leq E + \alpha$ there is no individual incentive to act unilaterally, and if no one contributes then for every agent the no contribution strategy is the best choice because by not contributing he gets $U_F = 0$, while by contributing he gets $U_C = G - (E + \alpha) \leq 0$.

The other type is any equilibrium where exactly m agents contribute and the remaining $N - m$ deviate. In fact, for each of the $N - m$ deviating agents the free riding strategy F is the best choice because he gets $U_F = G > U_C = G - \left(\dfrac{E}{m+1} + \alpha \right)$. At the same time, for each of the m contributing agents the contributing strategy C is the best choice. If he chooses to contribute he gets $U_C = G - (E/m + \alpha) > 0$. If he chooses to defect he gets $U_F = 0$ because his defection would cause also the remaining $m - 1$ to defect. Indeed, if one of the m contributing agents withdraws, the payoff of the remaining $m - 1$ becomes $U_C = G - \left(\dfrac{E}{m-1} + \alpha \right) \leq 0$ and they would all cease to contribute. There are therefore as many distinct NE with m agents contributing and $N - m$ defecting, as there are distinct m-sized subgroups.

However, a qualitatively important qualification is in order at this stage. Strictly, the existence of a *NE* where exactly *m* agents contribute *depends on the size of m*. The contributing subgroup may be *sufficiently small* as to make a single withdrawal clearly felt by the others, in the sense that they would find their contributing payoff to change from > 0 to ≤ 0, and decide to withdraw as well. But each contributing agent, taken separately, knows that since his withdrawal would cause everybody to withdraw, his best choice is to keep contributing. Alternatively, the contributing subgroup may be *sufficiently large* as to make the impact of a single withdrawal on the payoff of the remaining *m* − 1 negligible. Each contributing agent, taken separately, knows that since his withdrawal has no perceptible impact on the others' payoff, the others would keep contributing, and his own best choice becomes to withdraw. But this holds separately for each of them, and so the best choice for each becomes to withdraw. In other words, if *m* is sufficiently large any situation with *m* contributing agents would cease to be a *NE*, and the only *NE* would again be the (unique) one where no one contributes.

The strategic equilibria described above do provide – in their own right – some insight into the failures of collective action under free cooperation. However, they are introduced here *in primis* as a starting point for the study of the *dynamic repeated game RG* in the next section, and of the impact of the free riding incentive on the *insufficient* supply of *G* in the *SG* of the last section.

A repeated game of free cooperation: the role of group size and time discounting

We now consider a *repeated dynamic game RG*, consisting of an infinite repetition, over time $t = 0, 1, 2...$, of a *static game SG*. To deal with it we need to introduce a *(time) discount factor* δ, representing the weight given by individual agents to the future relative to the present. It is formally related to the *(time) rate of discount* r by the formula

$$\delta = \frac{1}{1+r} \tag{4}$$

$$r \in [0, \infty) \rightarrow \delta \in [1, 0)$$

represented graphically in Figure 2.1.

δ ranges between $1(r = 0)$ where the future has exactly the same weight as the present, and 0 ($r \rightarrow \infty$) where the future has no weight whatsoever compared to the present, so that an increase in δ, equivalent

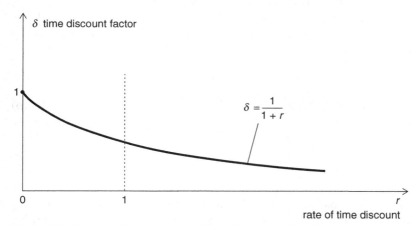

Figure 2.1 The time discount factor δ and the rate of time discount r

to a decrease in r, means an increase in the importance given to the future in comparison to the present. We have as before two individual strategies, C and F. But here these must be refined in terms of the infinite time horizon. We define a *dynamic contributing strategy* σ_C as one where agent i chooses C at $t = 0$, on the assumption that everybody else does the same, and then continues to choose C until he discovers that somebody has deviated by choosing F, in which case, starting from the next period $t+1$, he also chooses F forever. If he chooses C forever his discounted payoff is

$$V_C = \big(G - (E/N + \alpha)\big)(1 + \delta + \delta^2 + ..)$$

$$= \frac{1}{1-\delta}(G - (E/N + \alpha)) \tag{5}$$

$$\delta \in [0,1)$$

As before, we distinguish between the two alternatives $G \leq E/N + \alpha$ and $G > E/N + \alpha$. In the former the discounted payoff of the contributing agent is $V_C \leq 0$ for every δ, so that from the very start of the game no one chooses C and the only *NE* is no collective action. We therefore move on to the second alternative, the one that yields a positive $V_C > 0$ for every δ. Here we can introduce the alternative *dynamic non-contributing (free riding) strategy* σ_F where individual i chooses F at $t = 0$ and continues to do so forever. The free rider knows that in each period t there is a probability $p \in [0,1]$ that his free riding will be detected, and that if it is detected then starting from $t+1$ the collective action ceases forever. His discounted payoff is

$$V_F = G + \delta(1-p)G + \delta^2(1-p)^2 G + ..$$
$$= G(1 + \delta(1-p) + \delta^2(1-p)^2 + ..) \tag{6}$$
$$= \frac{1}{1-\delta(1-p)} G$$
$$\delta(1-p) \in [0,1)$$

The two alternative strategies imply that the dynamic contributing strategy σ_C – *by all players and from the beginning* – becomes the (unique) *NE* when the following *Incentive Compatibility Constraint ICC* is satisfied

$$V_C > V_F$$

$$\frac{1}{1-\delta}(G - (E/N + \alpha)) > \frac{1}{1-\delta(1-p)} G \tag{7}$$

$$G - (E/N + \alpha) > \frac{1-\delta}{1-\delta(1-p)} G$$

while the dynamic non-contributing strategy σ_F – *by all players from the beginning* – becomes the (unique) *NE* when $V_C \leq V_F$.

The crucial role in the *ICC* is played by the function

$$f(p,\delta) = \frac{1-\delta}{1-\delta(1-p)} \tag{8}$$

which we represent in Figure 2.2 as a function of δ for different values of p.

For any given p the function $f(\cdot,\delta)$ decreases in δ, ranging from $1(\delta=0)$ to 0 ($\delta=1$). The two boundary cases are the two thick straight lines shown in the figure: the downward-sloping one corresponding to $p=1$ and the kinked horizontal and vertical one corresponding to $p=0$.

Combining (7) with the shape of the function $f(\cdot,\delta)$ of (8) we see that for any p, as δ increases from 0 and to 1, the right-hand term of (7) decreases

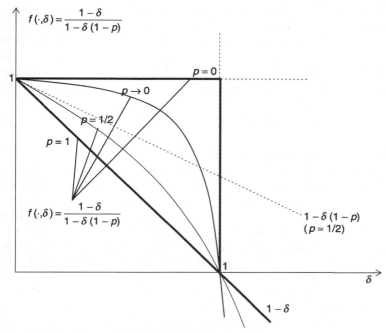

Figure 2.2 The shape of $f(\cdot,\delta)$ for different values of p

from $f(\cdot,0)G = G > G - (E/N + \alpha)$ to $f(\cdot,1)G = 0 < G - (E/N + \alpha)$, so that there exists some value $0 < \tilde{\delta} < 1$ which brings the left and right terms of (7) into equality. By rearranging terms we obtain this *critical time discount factor* $\tilde{\delta}$

$$G - (E/N + \alpha) = \frac{1-\delta}{1-\delta(1-p)}G \rightarrow \qquad (9)$$

$$\rightarrow \tilde{\delta} = \frac{1}{1 + \left(\dfrac{G}{E/N + \alpha} - 1\right)p}$$

as a function of $G, (E/N + \alpha)$ and p. As long as $\delta \leq \tilde{\delta}(\cdot)$ we have $V_C \leq V_F$ (the term on the right in (7) is greater than or equal to the term on the left). If people weigh the future less than or equally to the critical time discount factor $\tilde{\delta}(\cdot)$, then *free riding* from the very first period for ever

becomes the best choice *for every agent*. Free riding by all – and no collective action *G* – becomes the new (unique) *NE*. As soon as $\delta > \tilde{\delta}(\cdot)$ we
have $V_C > V_F$. If people weigh the future more than $\tilde{\delta}(\cdot)$, then *free contribution*, or *free cooperation*, from the very first period forever becomes
the best choice *for every agent*. Free cooperation by all in the collective
action *G* becomes the (unique) *NE*. The *ICC* for a contributing *NE* may
thus be restated as

$$\delta > \tilde{\delta}(G,(E \,/\, N + \alpha), p) \tag{10}$$

where $\tilde{\delta}(\cdot)$ is the function defined by (9).

We now introduce *two drastic assumptions*. They are effective in simplifying the algebra of the model, yet they are also perfectly acceptable
in relation to the model's level of abstraction. They allow us to bring to
the fore the factors impairing any free collective action in the pursuit of
common shared interests when these are open to the unrestrained possibility of free riding: the *size* of the group-community, and the *related
probability* of individual free riding being perceived/detected by the
group's members.

First, we assume a constant ratio $E \,/\, N = k$, i.e. a proportional relationship between the *production* cost *E* of providing a given amount-
quality of *G* and the size *N* of the group-community served by it: when
the size of the group doubles, the cost of providing the given amount-
quality of *G* to it doubles as well. Notice that a decrease in $(k + \alpha)$ for a
given *G* and an increase in *G* for a given $(k + \alpha)$ mean substantially the
same thing: an increase in the efficiency with which the group's common
interests are being satisfied. In the former case the same amount-quality
of *G* is provided at a lower cost per head. In the latter a higher amount-
quality of *G* is provided at the same cost per head. We mention this formally trivial difference because in the following derivations, specifically
in (12) and Figure 2.3, we see that changes in *G* or $(k + \alpha)$ have different
impacts on the equilibrium outcomes. As to the correct interpretation of
the proportionality assumption, to avoid confusion we further specify
its formal meaning. Given a group of agents and their shared common
interests, *G* is a measure of the level of satisfaction of such interests, or
equivalently the amount-quality of the group goods which satisfy them.
The idea underlying the proportionality assumption is that when the size
of the group increases, the cost of ensuring a *given level* of satisfaction of
the members' common interests, i.e. of providing a given amount-quality
of *G* (and associated individual benefit) to the group, increases in the
same proportion. Notice that since here the amount-quality of *G* is fixed

(no variable supply), such amount-quality and the associated individual benefit can formally be treated as variables independent from each other, and the same holds for G and its cost E (in the last section we shall see that when we want to investigate the game's outcome not on G yes or no, but on G's *level*, the individual benefit from G and the cost of G must both be treated as functions of G itself).

Second, we assume that the probability of an agent's free riding being perceived/detected is a *decreasing* function of N

$$p(N) \mid p_N' < 0, p(2) = 1 \quad \text{and} \quad p(N) \to 0 \quad \text{as} \quad N \to \infty \tag{11}$$

or else $p(N) = 0$ when N becomes very large, say $\bar{N}$

This probability decreases with the size of the group for two related but distinct reasons. As the group becomes larger, on one hand it becomes easier for the single agent to hide his deviating behaviour, and on the other the impact of a single agent's withdrawal on whatever collective action is being undertaken by the group is diminished. In the one-stage *SG* model of the section above and of the last one below, the distinction-relationship between these two aspects of an agent's deviating behaviour emerges explicitly, but here we lump them together into a simple function $p(N)$. When the group-community is very small, the probability of deviation being perceived/detected is unity (this is represented here in the extreme case of $N = 2$). As N increases, the probability of perception/detection decreases, at first slowly and then faster after the group-community exceeds a certain size, and then tends towards zero, or vanishes altogether, when the size becomes very large, such as in the case of a typical political community. Of course, *very small* and *very large* are here highly relative concepts, which depend on the nature of both the collective action and the group-community in question.

As a result, (9) becomes

$$\tilde{\delta} = \frac{1}{1 + \left(\dfrac{G}{k+a} - 1\right) p(N)} \tag{12}$$

$$= \tilde{\delta}(G, (k + \alpha), N)$$

The situation is depicted in Figure 2.3.

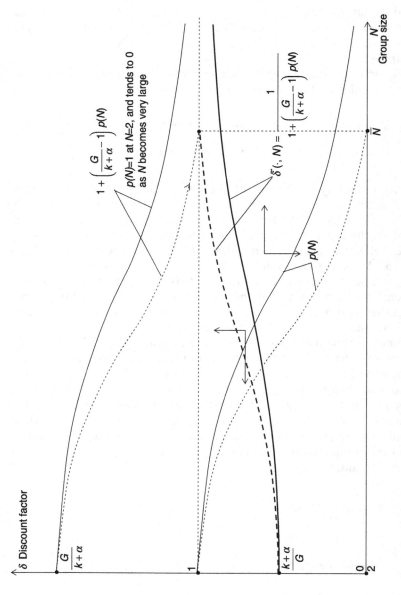

δ Discount factor

$\dfrac{G}{k+\alpha}$

$1 + \left(\dfrac{G}{k+\alpha} - 1 \right) p(N)$

$p(N) = 1$ at $N=2$, and tends to 0 as N becomes very large

1

$\delta(\cdot, N) = \dfrac{1}{1 + \left(\dfrac{G}{k+\alpha} - 1 \right) p(N)}$

$\dfrac{k+\alpha}{G}$

$p(N)$

0

2

$\bar{N}$

N Group size

Figure 2.3 The impact of a rising N on the critical discount factor

The dependence of $\tilde{\delta}(\cdot)$ from its arguments is immediately obvious from both (12) and the figure. The critical (time) discount factor decreases in G because an increase in G ceteris paribus means an increase in the individual net benefit. It increases in $(k+\alpha)$ because an increase in $(k+\alpha)$ ceteris paribus means a decrease in the individual net benefit. Finally, it increases in N because an increase in N means a decrease in the probability of free riding being perceived/detected. We see in particular in the figure that as $(k+\alpha)$ approaches G from below, the curve $\tilde{\delta}(\cdot, N)$ becomes ever more squeezed towards the horizontal line at height 1, and coincides with it when $G = (k+\alpha)$.

The results shown in (12) and in Figure 2.3 can be summarized as follows.

Given the structural properties of the particular collective action or group goods in question, i.e. its benefits and costs per head as well as the intrinsic unrestrained possibility of free riding on the group goods, under free cooperation and in the perspective of a long time horizon of repeated choices the relationship between the individual incentive to contribute and the individual incentive to free ride depends crucially on the probability of an agent's free riding being perceived/detected by the others, and on the relative importance given to the future in comparison to the present. The relative strength of the incentive to contribute over the incentive to free ride increases with the probability of free riding being perceived/detected and with the importance given to the future. On the other hand, since the probability of free riding being perceived/detected decreases indefinitely with the size of the group, when the group becomes very large the incentive to free ride tends to dominate over the incentive to contribute irrespective of the importance given to the future. All this is indicated by the arrows in Figure 2.3: increases in δ and decreases in N increase the relative strength of the incentive to contribute over the incentive to free ride, and vice versa. When the incentive to free ride dominates over the incentive to contribute, and this happens inevitably when the group-community becomes very large, the provision of G collapses. To the extent that the group's members perceive the collective action in question as essential for their general welfare, the fact that under free cooperation it would not be undertaken may be one of the reasons – though not necessarily the only or primary one – why the group itself evolves from an aggregation of free and independently acting people into an organization.

A repeated game of enforced cooperation under an organized group

We now assume a group whose members are not just an aggregation of agents who are free and independent from each other in all their actions, so that the satisfaction of their common shared interests rests on a purely voluntary interaction–cooperation with each other. The group-community is an *organization* in the sense that it is endowed with a governance structure, i.e. an internal system of power which enables it to enforce rules and behaviours upon its members, specifically to make a member's contributing to the cost of G into a *social obligation* whose violation is *socially sanctioned* by a penalty. In general we may think of such a group as *any* kind of *organized* collection of people bound together by *any* kind of shared interests.

We substitute the free interaction cost per head α with an *organization cost* per person β, the administrative-bureaucratic cost of running the organization itself, as distinct from the direct (production) cost of providing G, while $E, N, E/N = k$ are the same as before. Each member is required to contribute $(k + \beta)$ to the cost of G and defection is sanctioned by a penalty P, which we compute in money terms, but may also take other forms of social condemnation. The probability p of a member's violation being detected by the organization is assumed to be independent of the group's size N (the cost of detecting defections certainly increases with the size of the group, but here it is coherently included in β) and constant over time. If a member does not pay his due in period t, and is detected, then he will be forced to pay P in period $t + 1$. The organization keeps providing G to the whole group independently of whether one or more members choose to comply or to defect, so that choosing to defect means simply choosing to free ride on the provision of G.

In this scenario the group's members no longer play strategies with each other. A strategy is played by each member not with the others but with the organization, with an asymmetry that highly simplifies the game. Each member has a choice between a *dynamic repeated complying strategy* σ_C and a *dynamic repeated non-complying (free riding, defecting) strategy* σ_F, each of which entails a well-defined payoff. The organization does not have to choose between alternative strategies. It has a single strategy, consisting in imposing the penalty P on every defecting and detected member.

We have a *dynamic repeated complying strategy* σ_C when an agent i chooses C (comply) at $t = 0$ and continues to do so forever. His discounted payoff is therefore

$$V_C = (G - (k + \beta))(1 + \delta + \delta^2 + ..) \tag{13}$$

$$= \frac{1}{1 - \delta}(G - (k + \beta))$$

We have a *dynamic repeated non-complying strategy* σ_F when an agent i chooses F (free ride) at $t = 0$ and continues to do so forever. The organization keeps providing G but sanctions the members whose defection in t is detected with P to be paid in $t + 1$. The discounted payoff of this agent is therefore

$$V_F = G + (G - pP)(\delta + \delta^2 + ..) \tag{14}$$

$$= G + \frac{\delta}{1 - \delta}(G - pP)$$

where pP is the expected penalty.

The *Incentive Compatibility Constraint ICC* is formally the same as before, with

$$V_C > V_F \tag{15}$$

for a complying *NE*, and $V_C \leq V_F$ for a non-complying *NE*.

By rearranging and simplifying terms the *ICC* yields the condition

$$pP\delta > k + \beta \tag{16}$$

which in turn yields the *critical discount factor* $\hat{\delta}$

$$pP\delta = k + \beta \rightarrow$$

$$\rightarrow \hat{\delta} = \frac{k + \beta}{pP} \tag{17}$$

$$= \hat{\delta}\big((k + \beta), pP\big)$$

as a function of $(k + \beta)$ and pP. As long as $\delta \leq \hat{\delta}(\cdot)$ we have $V_C \leq V_F$ and no complying from the beginning forever becomes the best choice for every agent. As soon as $\delta > \hat{\delta}(\cdot)$ we have $V_C > V_F$ and complying from the

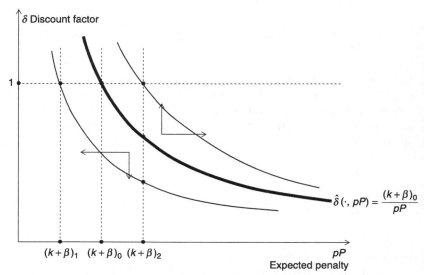

Figure 2.4 Enforced cooperation: the role of the expected penalty pP

beginning forever becomes the best choice for every agent. The *ICC* for a complying *NE* may thus be restated as

$$\delta > \hat{\delta}((k+\beta), pP) \tag{18}$$

The situation is depicted in Figure 2.4 and the results shown in (17) and in the figure can be summarized as follows.

To say that an organization can impose upon its members the obligation to contribute to the cost of the group goods is the same thing as to say that it has the power to sanction free riding by imposing upon free riders the payment of a penalty. Given the structural properties of the group goods, i.e. its benefits and costs per head as well as the intrinsic unrestrained possibility of free riding on the group goods, under enforced cooperation and in the perspective of a long time horizon of repeated choices the relationship between the individual incentive to comply and the individual incentive to not comply (free ride) depends crucially on the value attributed to the expected penalty, which depends on the amount and nature of the penalty and the probability of defection being detected by the organization, and on the relative importance given to the future in comparison to the present. The relative strength of the incentive to comply over the incentive to free ride increases with the excess of the expected penalty over the *obligatory payment and with the importance given to the future. When the expected penalty is the same as the obligatory payment the incentive to free ride dominates over the incentive to comply irrespective of the importance given to the future. All this is indicated by the arrows in Figure 2.4: increases in δ and pP for given $k + \beta$ increase the relative strength of the incentive to comply over the incentive to free ride, and vice versa. When the incentive to free ride dominates the incentive to comply the organization keeps providing the group goods because it is its responsibility to do so, while imposing the penalty on the detected free riders. However, this is a state that cannot endure. It means that the organization is not functioning, and if it is incapable of reversing the situation it is unlikely to survive.*

In comparing the *NE* under enforced cooperation with those under free cooperation there are a number of significant social aspects, both formal and substantial, that we want to emphasize.

The main social difference is that under free cooperation free riding is a socially legitimate choice subject to no social sanction, and it may well lead to no provision of *G*. Under enforced cooperation free riding is a socially sanctioned violation of a social obligation, which does not lead to no *G* because the organization is there precisely to ensure its provision.

Under enforced cooperation the critical (time) discount factor $\hat{\delta}$ depends only on the cost of *G* per head ($k + \beta$) and the expected penalty. It depends neither on *G* itself nor on the size *N* of the group, as it does instead under free cooperation. This is due to the simple fact that under the assumptions of the model in the case of enforced cooperation the prevalence $V_F > V_C$ of the discounted net benefit from free riding (14) over the discounted net benefit from contributing (13) does not depend on *G*, and *p* does not depend on *N*, whereas in the case of free cooperation (6, 5) they both do.

In Figure 2.4 if the point (δ, pP) lies to the right of the curve $\hat{\delta}(\cdot)$ then we have a *NE* where *G* is provided, all members of the group choose to comply, and there are no violators on whom to impose *P*. If it lies on $\hat{\delta}(\cdot)$ or to its left, then we have a *NE* where *G* is still provided (contrary to the collapse of *G* under free cooperation), but all members choose not to comply, and the organization has to impose *P* on those who are caught. Looking beyond the model's formal expressions, into the actual nature of social organizations, it is clear that only a condition relatively close to the former state is socially sustainable. A condition closer to the latter state must be viewed as a pathological, socially unsustainable condition. If the organization is to be viable and survive it will have to be capable to shift the point (δ, pP) to the right of $\hat{\delta}(\cdot)$, either by inducing people to give more weight to the future (an increase in δ), or by increasing pP (acting on either p or P), or by reducing $(k + \beta)$.

In order to give special emphasis to the kind of common shared interests playing the central role in this book, we further specify that in presenting and discussing the results of our formal analysis our implicit 'mental' reference is to certain socially well-defined types of group-communities, common shared interests, and enforcing authorities: (i) not any type of group-community, but a *political-civic* community, also referred to in the universal language of Western political thought as a *civitas*, (ii) not any type of common shared interests, but the common interests which the members of the *civitas* share in their capacity as its *citizens*, and which only by virtue of this special property deserve the name of *public* interests, and (iii) not any type of enforcing authority, but a *government authority* having the *political power* of imposing rules and enforcing behaviours upon its citizens. Under such interpretation we think of β as the bureaucratic-administrative cost of running government institutions, as distinct from the direct (production) cost of providing G. As for G, it represents a given amount-quality of *public* goods (and the associated individual benefit derived from them), i.e. a given level of satisfaction of the citizens' *public* interests, while N is the population of the political community. The individual mandatory payment of $(k + \beta)$ and the individual choice to defect on it are therefore to be interpreted, the former as the *tax liability* per head, and the latter as the *public free riding* par excellence, namely the individual choice to defect on the fiscal obligation. The government's authority to make taxes into socially mandatory payments is one and the same thing with its authority to impose a penalty on the citizens whose free riding is detected. The two are actually distinct expressions of a single authority, the strength of one is the strength of the other, and such strength is in turn tightly dependent on the capacity of the political ruling class to pursue the actual shared interests of the citizens instead of the rent interests of special subgroups of society. To the extent that this authority weakens, the underlying organized political-civic community shifts into a non-organized community intrinsically impaired in its capacity of collective action.

The fading of collective action in a one-stage game of free cooperation

We now resume the static one-stage game of free cooperation of the corresponding section above. Our purpose is to adjust the model to make it fit for investigating the effect of the group size not only on whether

G will be provided or not (as in that section), but also on the *level* of its provision, specifically on a *less than efficient level of satisfaction of the group's common shared interests*. We present the argument entirely in graphical terms, taking as our starting point a graphic analysis used to prove the important result that in a group of two people and a common good G, under free cooperation the *Nash equilibrium NE* supply G_{NE} is *less* than the efficient so called *Lindahl equilibrium LE* supply G_{LE}. It is a graphic analysis that can currently be found in standard microeconomics textbooks. The one from which we take it is by Andrew Schotter (2009: Fig. 25.3, p. 643), where the reader can also find references to the original papers dealing with the topic under various perspectives. The diagram in our Figure 2.5 is basically an adaptation of Schotter's diagram to the case of two equal representative agents. Although the diagram can be drawn for *any* pair of *different* agents, each with his or her own particular preferences over public versus private consumption, we adapt it to the assumption of identical representative agents, and draw all its schedules as straight lines purely for graphical simplicity. The assumption of representative agents, already used in the rest of the chapter, is maintained here because it is particularly useful for our subsequent graphical generalization, and causes no serious losses of meaning.

On the horizontal axis we measure the (variable) amount-quality of G. On the vertical axis we measure the cost share s of agent A, whose unitary complement $(1-s)$ is the cost share of agent B. The indifference curves of A in the space (G,s) have the particular shape drawn in the figure, convex towards the top and corresponding to increasing levels of utility as they move downwards. The indifference curves of B are drawn in the same way, except that they are turned upside down. With the sole purpose of easing the interpretation of Figure 2.5 we add here Figure 2.6 which is self-explanatory because it is the conventional depiction of how to construct the demand for G using changing individual budget lines (c is individual private consumption, y individual gross income, $f(G)$ the total (nonlinear) cost function of G, and s the individual cost share). The link to Figure 2.5 is in the top panel, while in the bottom panel is the link to Figure 2.7, to be used later. To highlight the link to Figure 2.5 we have selected a set of elements: one indifference curve u_0, with three points on it, $P_0, 0, P_0$, and two cost shares, s_0, s_2. They have the same meaning and label in both diagrams, and with their one–one correspondence they show how the diagram in Figure 2.5 is derived from the top diagram in Figure 2.6. Needless to say, the correspondence between the diagrams is 'qualitative' and no attempt is made to preserve 'quantitative' correspondence. Returning to Figure 2.5 we see that the downward

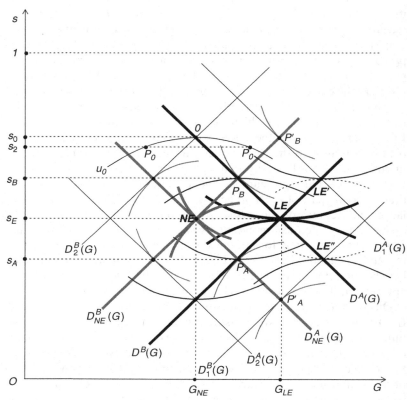

Figure 2.5 Inefficiency of the Nash equilibrium

sloping thick black line labelled $D^A(G)$ joining the highest points of the family of A's indifference curves is to be interpreted as representing A's *actually* desired levels of G for decreasing levels of his cost share s, and the same meaning holds, with inverted direction along the s axis, for the upward sloping thick black line labelled $D^B(G)$, relative to agent B. The intersection point **LE** (Lindahl equilibrium) of the two lines, with tangent indifference curves, corresponds to the efficient level G_{LE}. While the thick black lines represent the actual preferences of the two agents, the thick grey ones are to be interpreted as Nash *best reply functions*. They are built on the obvious assumption that each agent does not know what the actual preferences of the other are. He might ask, but since he cannot know whether the answers are truthful all he can do

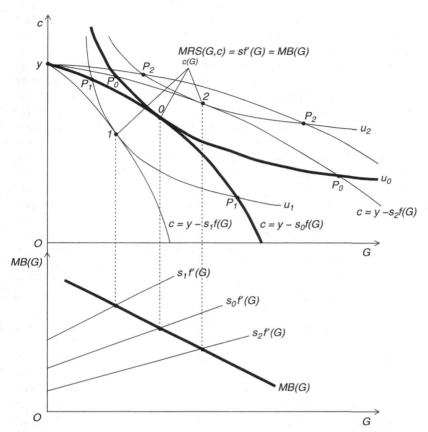

Figure 2.6 Individual cost shares, budget constraints and marginal benefit schedule

is to chose his best action for each possible preference structure of the other. This yields a precise interpretation of point P_B. It represents the best choice of agent B if the actual preferences of agent A were represented by the curve $D^A(G)$. This is indicated by the fact that point P_B is where the highest indifference curve of B is tangent to the curve $D^A(G)$, with $B's$ contributing share $1 - s_B$ being lower than his contributing share $1 - s_E$ at the Lindahl equilibrium point ***LE*** (remembering that a rise along the vertical s-axis means a decrease in $B's$ contributing share). If the actual preference of A is represented by the curve $D^A(G)$, then for B points on higher indifference curves are unattainable while points on lower indifference curves would not be the best choice. But if $A's$ actual preference were represented not by $D^A(G)$ but by $D_1^A(G)$, then $B's$ best choice would be at point P_B'. Joining all points like P_B and P_B' tangent to all possible $D^A(G)$ curves we obtain the upward sloping thick grey line labelled $D_{NE}^B(G)$ representing the best reply function of agent B for all possible preferences of agent A. If we proceed to similarly determine the best choices of agent A for all possible preferences $D^B(G)$ of agent B, we obtain points P_A (with $A's$ contributing share s_A lower than his contributing share s_E at point LE) and P_A', and then the downward sloping thick grey line labelled $D_{NE}^A(G)$, representing the best reply function of agent A for all possible preferences of agent B. The intersection point NE of these two thick grey curves is the Nash equilibrium. It is clear that the Nash equilibrium point NE must lie to the left of the Lindahl equilibrium point LE, which implies the already mentioned important result $G_{NE} < G_{LE}$. In words, the Nash equilibrium leads *necessarily* to an inefficiently low level of G. The inefficiency gap $G_{LE} - G_{NE}$, though always positive, may vary depending on the structure of the two agents' preferences, which of course will in general differ from one another. Here the many symmetries appearing in the diagram, in particular the fact that the equilibrium cost share s_E remains the same under the Lindahl and Nash equilibria, are accidental, in the sense that they are simply a consequence of our assumption of equal representative agents. In general with different agents the symmetries would disappear.

Having reproduced in full the standard graphical proof of the result $G_{NE} < G_{LE}$ in the two agents case, we now embark on the specific purpose of this section, which is to investigate how the result is affected by an indefinite increase in the size of the group. Following intuition, it is a relatively simple matter to rigorously prove that when the group size N increases, the NE equilibrium level G_{NE} decreases steadily, approaching zero as N increases indefinitely. In other words, as the group size increases, the incentive to *freely cooperate* for the provision of the group's common shared interests weakens, and tends to vanish completely when the group becomes very large. Correspondingly, the complement incentive to free ride becomes stronger, until it remains the only one. This fact is intuitive, but we prove it formally in the simplest game-theoretic framework.

Now, Figure 2.5 does not allow us to search for the effect of an increase in N because by construction it cannot accommodate more than two agents. We therefore need to convert the argument developed in Figure 2.5 into its equivalent in Figure 2.7 which instead does allow us to see what happens when we multiply at pleasure the number N of representative agents. It must, however, be noted again that while distances,

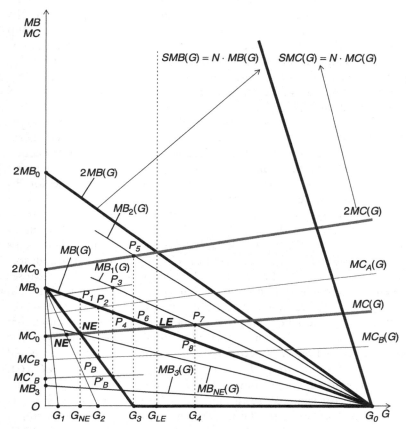

Figure 2.7 From small to large groups

points, and slopes shown in the figure are 'qualitatively' accurate, we make no claim to full 'quantitative' accuracy. To start with, we consider also in Figure 2.7 only two identical (representative) agents, labelled A, B. On the horizontal axis we measure the amount-quality of G and on the vertical axis its individual and social marginal benefits and costs. In the one-stage game section above we assumed a fixed amount G, a fixed uniform individual benefit from G, normalized to be equal to G itself, and a fixed cost E of providing G, divided into equal parts among the N members of the group. We now revise these assumptions as follows. (i) Since the amount-quality of G is variable, we assume a uniform individual marginal benefit schedule $MB(G)$ (see bottom panel of Figure 2.6 for its construction), so that the social marginal benefit schedule becomes $SMB(G) = 2\,MB(G)$. (ii) We assume a *basic* marginal cost schedule $MC(G)$ representing the marginal cost of providing G in the purely 'benchmark' state of a group consisting of only one member. (iii) The more general assumption is – as in the preceding sections on repeated games – that the cost of providing G increases in proportion with the number of group members, so that the social marginal cost schedule of providing G to the two agents A, B is $SMC(G) = 2\,MC(G)$.

The efficient Lindahl equilibrium level of G is of course at point **LE**, with amount G_{LE}. But here enters the simple strategy already described in Figure 2.5. In this Figure 2.7, let the curve $MB(G)$ represent the actual preferences of agent A, and let us look, by reasoning on the diagram, for what would be the best contributing choice by agent B, i.e. for $B's$ contributing choice that would maximize his net payoff under $A's$ given preference. Clearly the contributing choice of point **LE** with equal cost shares $MC(G)$ is not the best. $B's$ payoff (equal to $A's$ payoff) is measured by the area $MB_0 - LE - MC_0$, but it is clear that if B reduces his cost share his payoff increases. The graphical reasoning is straightforward. Starting at point **LE**, a marginal reduction in $B's$ cost share causes an equal complementary marginal rise in $A's$ cost share. For notational clarity we therefore now indicate the two complementary cost shares with the separate labels $MC_A(G)$ and $MC_B(G)$, keeping in mind that at point **LE** they both coincide with the equal cost share $MC(G)$. The marginal reduction in $B's$ cost share gives him a marginal gain equal to the *flat distance* $MC_0 - LE$ along his marginal cost curve $MC_B(G)$, which at point **LE** coincides with $MC(G)$. The complementary marginal rise in $A's$ cost share causes a marginal leftward shift (decrease) in G away from G_{LE}, to ensure the maintenance of the behavioural equilibrium condition of equality between $A's$ marginal benefit curve $MB(G)$ and his marginal cost curve $MC_A(G)$ (which, as just noted, at point **LE** coincides with $MC(G)$). This marginal leftward shift in G causes in turn a marginal loss to B equal to the *vertical distance* between his $MB(G)$ curve and his $MC_B(G)$ cost curve. At point **LE** this vertical distance is equal to zero because $MC_B(G) = MC(G)$. Thus, starting at point **LE** a marginal reduction in $B's$ cost share causes a net increase in his payoff equal to the flat distance $MC_0 - LE$ along his marginal cost curve $MC_B(G) = MC(G)$. As we see in the diagram, as B continues to lower his contributing cost share the complementary contributing cost share by A continues to rise by an equal amount, G continues to shift leftwards to ensure the maintenance of $A's$ required behavioural equilibrium condition, and $B's$ payoff continues to increase as long as the (decreasing) flat distance along his downward sliding marginal cost curve $MC_B(G)$

is greater than the (increasing) vertical distance between his marginal benefit curve $MB(G)$ and such downward sliding marginal cost curve. As shown in the diagram, $B's$ payoff reaches its maximum when these two distances become equal, i.e. when a further reduction in his cost share ceases to increase his payoff. This happens at point P_B, with cost shares $MC_B(G)$ and $MC_A(G)$ respectively. P_B is therefore the best contributing choice of B under $A's$ given preference represented by the $MB(G)$ curve. It should be noted that the *black thick line* joining the points $MB_0 - G_3$ is drawn precisely so that at each of its points the vertical distance to the $MB(G)$ curve and the flat distance to the vertical axis along the downward sliding marginal cost curve $MC_B(G)$ are equal. Now consider the family of all possible 'demand' curves of A, $MB_A(G)$, obtained by rotating the initial curve $MB(G)$ around point G_0. By rotating it clockwise or anticlockwise we represent higher or lower demands by A, respectively. In view of our remaining discussion we have drawn three such different demands by A, labelled $MB_1(G), MB_2(G), MB_3(G)$, respectively. As in Figure 2.5, agent B does not know what the actual preferences of A are. He will therefore have a best contributing choice (share) for each of the possible 'demands' by A. By applying the same type of graphical reasoning developed so far we can construct the family of all such best contributing shares, and show that $B's$ *best reply function* consisting of all those best choices is represented in the diagram by the *black thick broken line* joining points $MB_0 - G_3 - G_0$. To prove this last proposition we apply, by way of example, the previous graphical reasoning to the identification of the following three further points P_B', G_3 and MB_0 lying on the black broken line. It can be easily verified that if the demand by A were not the curve $MB(G)$ but the (higher) curve $MB_1(G)$, then the best contributing choice by B would move from point P_B to point P_B'. Let us start with B choosing again the equal contributing share $MC(G)$. He would find himself at point P_7, with a net payoff equal to the area $MB_0 - LE - MC_0$ minus the area $LE - P_7 - P_8$. Clearly by reducing his contributing share his marginal net gain would be largely positive, being equal to the flat distance $MC_0 - P_7$ plus the vertical distance $P_7 - P_8$ (measuring a negative marginal loss because the marginal benefit is less than the marginal cost). If he continues to reduce his contributing share he would continue to increase his payoff, until he reaches point P_B'. At this point his contributing share is given by the marginal cost curve starting at point MC_B', and his payoff is given by the area $MB_0 - P_4 - P_B' - MB_B'$. He has no incentive to further decrease his contribution because by construction this is the point where his marginal gain, given by the flat distance $MC_B' - P_B'$, is equal to his marginal loss given by the vertical distance $P_4 - P_B'$. By the same logic we see that if the demand by A were the even higher curve $MB_2(G)$, then $B's$ best contributing choice would be to not contribute at all. The whole cost would be borne by A (point P_5) and B would find himself at point G_3. By construction, at this point if he *increased* his contributing share his marginal *loss*, given by the flat distance $O - G_3$, would be equal to his marginal gain, given by the vertical distance $P_6 - G_3$. Finally consider the limiting case represented by point MB_0 on the vertical axis. This is $B's$ best contributing choice if $A's$ demand were the (lower) curve $MB_3(G)$. We have drawn this curve so as to let the vertical distance $MB_3 - O$ on the vertical axis to be equal to the vertical distance $2MC_0 - MB_0$ on the same vertical axis. This means that $B's$ contributing share required to induce A to supply some G must be higher than at point MB_0, because it is only in this case that $A's$ contributing share would be lower than at point MB_3. But with a contributing share higher than MB_0 and a positive G, $B's$ payoff would be negative. It follows that if we start with $B's$ contributing share higher than MB_0 and a positive G, it would be to the advantage of B to reduce this contributing share, because by doing so his payoff would increase (his negative payoff would decrease in absolute value). $B's$ best choice would be attained when his contributing share reaches MB_0 and G becomes zero.

We have thus shown that in this graphical model, if we take a group of two equal (representative) agents A and B, their *equal* best reply function is given by the black thick broken line joining points $MB_0 - G_3 - G_0$. The intersection point NE of the line with the equal cost share curve $MC(G)$ is the Nash equilibrium. It must obviously lie to the left of the Lindahl equilibrium point LE. It corresponds to an *assumed* equal demand curve $MB_A(G) = MB_B(G) = MB_{NE}(G)$ which is lower than the actual one $MB(G)$, and to an equilibrium payoff equal to the area $MB_0 - P_1 - NE - MC_0$, which is smaller than the area $MB_0 - LE - MC_0$ of the Lindahl equilibrium payoff at point LE.

We want now to see what happens when the group size increases. Suppose there are *three* agents A, B, C, with the same marginal benefit and cost curves $MB(G), MC(G)$ as before. Consider one agent, say C, and construct his best contributing shares in this new situation. This time, when C marginally reduces his cost share the complementary marginal increase in the cost share of the other two is distributed in *half* among them. This means that also the marginal reduction in G to ensure the maintenance of their behavioural equilibrium condition is reduced by $1/2$. This implies in turn also that $C's$ marginal loss in payoff due to this marginal decrease in G is reduced by $1/2$. By applying this reasoning to the diagram we see that in order to find $C's$ best reply function the (black) downward sloping line starting from point MB_0 must be steeper than the one holding for a group of only two. When the marginal decrease in G caused by a marginal reduction in $C's$ cost share is reduced by $1/2$ the equality between his marginal gain generated by his cost share reduction, and his marginal loss generated by the decrease in G is reached when the flat distance along $C's$ marginal cost curve is equal not to the vertical distance between this marginal cost curve and his marginal benefit curve, but to *half that distance*. Thus the slope of the (black) downward sloping line of the new best reply function, drawn thin in the diagram, must be such that at each of its points the flat distance, along $C's$ marginal cost curve, between the vertical axis and the intersection point of the cost curve with the line itself, is equal to half the vertical distance between this intersection point and the $MB(G)$ curve. The reason for this is of course intuitive. If a single agent reduces his cost share, the impact of the reduction on the cost shares borne by the other agents depends on their number. The greater is their number the smaller is the complementary increase in *their* cost shares. The smaller is the increase in their cost shares, the smaller is the equilibrium decrease in G, which is a non-rival shared good. And the smaller is the equilibrium decrease in G the smaller is the agent's loss in payoff caused by that decrease.

Now, agent C does not know the actual 'demand' curves of the other two agents. We must therefore consider the family of all their possible 'demand' curves. For the sake of simplicity we suppose all their individual demands to remain equal to each other, so that we may envisage the rotation of a single other demand $MB(G)$ around point G_0, as in the previous case of two agents, only with the understanding that this single demand must be multiplied by two. To each such new single demand, multiplied by two, there corresponds $C's$ best contributing choice, and the set of all these forms the *new steeper best reply function* joining points $MB_0 - G_2 - G_0$. Since this is the best reply function of each one of the three representative agents, its intersection point NE' with the $MC(G)$ curve – lying necessarily to the left of point NE – is the new Nash equilibrium of this three-member group. As the number N of agents continues to increase the $SMB(G) = N \cdot MB(G)$ curve rotates clockwise, the $SMC(G) = N \cdot MC(G)$ curve shifts and rotates upwards, and the point LE remains unchanged, but the individual best reply function, together with its Nash equilibrium intersection with the $MC(G)$ curve, becomes ever steeper, moving ever closer to the vertical axis.

In words, the results of this graphic analysis may be summarized as follows.

When the size of a community increases, the impact of a single agent's reduction in his contributory share to the cost of the community's common interests on the complementary contributory shares of the other members becomes ever smaller. As a consequence the single agent's incentive to increase his individual benefit by reducing his contributory share, i.e. by free riding on the others' contribution, becomes ever stronger, and the corresponding incentive to keep contributing becomes ever weaker. When the community becomes very large the individual incentive of each member to share in the cost of the community's common interests collapses, the corresponding incentive of each member to free ride is the only one to survive, and to the extent that the community's condition remains one of pure free cooperation no action to provide for its common interests will any longer be undertaken.

References

Abreu, D. 1988. 'On the Theory of Infinitely Repeated Games with Discounting'. *Econometrica*, 56: 383–96.

Abreu, D., Dutta, P. K., and Smith, L. 1994. 'The Folk Theorem for Repeated Games: A NEU Condition'. *Econometrica*, 62: 934–48.

Abreu, D., Pearce, D., and Stacchetti, E. 1986. 'Optimal Cartel Equilibria with Imperfect Monitoring'. *Journal of Economic Theory*, 39: 251–69.

Olson, M. 1965. *The Logic of Collective Action: Public Goods and the Theory of Groups*. Cambridge, MA: Harvard University Press.

Olson, M. 1987. 'Collective Action', in J. Eatwell, M. Milgate and P. Newman (eds.), *The New Palgrave: A Dictionary of Economics*. Basingstoke: Palgrave Macmillan.

Olson, M. 1996. 'Big Bills Left on the Sidewalk: Why Some Nations are Rich, and Others Poor'. *Journal of Economic Perspectives*, 10(2): 3–24.

Schotter, A. 2009. *Microeconomics: A Modern Approach*. Mason, OH: South Western.

Wen, Q. 1994. 'The Folk Theorem for Repeated Games with Complete Information'. *Econometrica*, 62: 949–54.

3 Internalizing environmental externalities

From deterministic to stochastic social damage

Manuela Coromaldi and Stefano Gorini

Introduction

This chapter deals with the problem of *internalizing* environmental externalities, with particular emphasis on the transition from *deterministic* to *stochastic production* externalities. The problem is introduced in the next section by presenting a formal and graphical analysis of a simple model of *consumption externalities*, intended to show what very complex features an ideal externality-based price system should possess. We then turn, in the section on deterministic externalities, to production externalities, where a rich literature has been confined to a deterministic setting. Classical environmental economic policy was developed around externalities created with relative certainty, like CO_2 emissions, pollution caused by waste disposal, and the like. Using a similarly simple model we discuss in formal and graphical terms the standard properties of the *partial internalization mechanism* of *deterministic production externalities*, based on the cost-minimizing incentive embedded in the creation of an artificial market for pollution permits. But in many important cases the externalities generated by production activities have a random nature, as with oil spills from tanker ships and offshore platforms, chemical and nuclear plant accidents, leakages from hazardous waste dumps, livestock disease outbreaks of avian or swine flu, and the like. In such cases of stochastic social damage, social cost minimization through the creation of a market for pollution permits becomes inapplicable. Keeping the simple procedure of the preceding sections, in the one on stochastic externalities we show that the problem of social cost minimization must be treated at company/industry level, because the only way to reduce the social cost of such activities is to devise company/industry specific incentives, aimed at reducing their particular environmental riskiness.

We then move on, in the section on oil spills, to a more detailed treatment of the particular stochastic externalities due to oil spills and other similar large-scale environmental accidents, based on the specialized literature, and in the section on optimal regulation we discuss the optimal regulation of stochastically polluting industries. The market-oriented approach to correct such externalities is to internalize social costs by requiring a stochastic polluter to repair any damage caused to others. Since the seminal paper by Becker (1968), economists have studied the optimal penalty for environmental damages, and as suggested by the literature and summarized in the simple framework of the section on stochastic externalities, also stochastic externalities can in principle be addressed using the rule of equating marginal benefits with marginal costs. However, though the rule is conceptually simple, it is often necessary to adapt it to the special difficulties of the actual cases, in particular when the environmental damage cannot be precisely and fully determined, and/or the costs to be sustained are just too high. Concluding remarks are summarized in the last section.

Special properties of externality-based price systems

Although the focus of this chapter is on *production* externalities, we begin it with a concise analysis of the case of *consumption* externalities because this allows us to highlight certain aspects of the problem of internalizing externalities into the price system, which are of such general significance that they may, under particular circumstances, apply also to the case of production externalities. We know the role of the price system in a commercial economy (an economy of rival interests/ commodities) with no externalities: under ideal and very restrictive conditions, of which the most important ones are the absence of market power and informational asymmetries, it ensures that the allocation of resources continuously gravitates towards some Pareto efficient state. But if we consider an *externality-generating type of (consumption or production) economic activity* then this ideal competitive price system would no longer ensure gravitation towards the two standard efficiency conditions, the one concerning the *total amount* of the activity, and the other concerning *the distribution of such total amount among* the individual agents. Let us define an *externality-based price system* as one that would be capable of *internalizing* the externality in question, by which we mean a price system that, under the above ideal conditions, would still pull the economy towards efficiency. It turns out that such an externality-based price system is as easy to be conceived in theory as it is difficult to be implemented in practice. In fact, depending on the particular circumstances, its practical implementation may simply be impossible. However, the difficulty/impossibility of practical implementation does not detract in the least from the importance of pointing out where exactly the inefficiencies of a *non-externality-based price system* would be located.

As anticipated, a fully externality-based price system ought to ensure two things. First, that the *total amount* of the externality-generating activity be the efficient one, i.e. that its social marginal benefit *SMB* be equal to its social marginal cost *SMC*. Second, that such total amount be *efficiently distributed* among the individual agents, i.e. that the *SMB* of the activity by agent i be the same as that by agent j, and that both be equal to the *SMC*. The second requirement implies that the prices faced by different agents must in general be different from one another. Our analysis follows Varian (1992: 438–9), but it introduces a necessary extension into the model. To maximize simplicity Varian considers only a pure exchange economy, but in this way the results are incomplete, and it is difficult to give them an intuitive and graphical interpretation. Without loss of simplicity, these limitations vanish if we move from an exchange to a production economy. Consider the simplest possible production model, with two private commodities Q and Y, and n consumers. Assume that individual consumption of Y (chosen as the numeraire) causes no externality, while individual consumption of Q does. In principle the externality may be positive or negative. The difference does not appear in the formalism, but in the graphical illustration we shall assume the externality to be negative, in order to stay closer to the chapter's emphasis on environmental pollution. We introduce this type of externality by assuming that each individual utility u_i depends on y_i and on the full vector (q_k) of the individual consumptions of Q:

$$u_i((q_k), y_i) \quad i, k = 1 \ldots n \tag{1}$$

Then we introduce a standard production constraint

$$F(Q, Y) = 0 \tag{2}$$

$$\sum_k q_k = Q, \quad \sum_i y_i = Y$$

and a standard social welfare function

$$W = \sum_i u_i((q_k), y_i) \tag{3}$$

The efficiency conditions for this economy are obtained by applying the usual formal optimization procedure.

1. Social optimization

$$\max_{q_k,y_i} \sum_i u_i((q_k),y_i) \ \text{s. to } F(Q,Y)=0 \tag{4}$$

2. Lagrangean

$$L(\cdot)=\sum_i u_i((q_k),y_i)-\lambda F(Q,Y) \tag{5}$$

FOC stage 1

1 eq : $\quad L'_\lambda(\cdot)=0 \rightarrow F(Q,Y)=0$

n eqs : $\quad L'_{q_k}(\cdot)=0 \rightarrow \sum_i MU_{iq_k}(\cdot)=\lambda F'_Q, \quad k=1...n \tag{6}$

n eqs : $\quad L'_{y_i}(\cdot)=0 \rightarrow MU_{iy_i}(\cdot)=\lambda F'_Y, \quad i=1...n$

FOC stage 2

1 eq : $\quad F(Q,Y)=0 \tag{7}$

n eqs : $\quad \sum_i \dfrac{MU_{iq_k}(\cdot)}{MU_{iy_i}(\cdot)}=\sum_i MRS_{y_i(q_k)\,i}(\cdot)=\dfrac{F'_Q}{F'_Y}$

$$= MRT_{Y(Q)}(\cdot), \quad k=1...r \tag{8}$$

n−1 eqs : $\quad MU_{iy_i}(\cdot)=MU_{jy_j}(\cdot), \quad \forall i,j \tag{9}$

FOC stage 3

1 eq : $\quad F(Q,Y)=0 \tag{10}$

n eqs : $\quad \sum_i MRS_{y_i(q_k)\,i}(\cdot)\equiv\sum_i MB_{iq_k}(\cdot)\equiv SMB_{q_k}(\cdot)=$

$$= MRT_{Y(Q)}(\cdot), k=1...n$$

The *FOC* stage 3 contain $1+n$ equations in the $2n$ variables (q_k,y_i), and with $n>1$ they yield the usual infinite set of efficient allocations (q_k^*,y_i^*), differing from each other in the distribution of welfare among the individuals. Eqs (8) show the existence of a fundamental kinship between externalities and public goods, but also of a fundamental difference. In the perspective of this book public goods stand for the public interests shared by the members of a political community, and exist independently of the simultaneous existence of the rival interests forming the texture of the commercial economy. Externalities are instead by their very nature a peculiar pathology, in fact the main pathology, of the commercial economy, which they need for their existence because it is in the commercial economy that rival interests are satisfied through exchange transactions between individual agents. At the same time, if we consider in particular the negative externalities lumped together in the general denomination of environmental pollution, they can for all purposes be treated as *negative* public goods, or *public bads*. It is precisely because of this peculiar combination of kinship/difference with public goods that externalities call for a special role of public policies and more generally government enforced cooperation to prevent the commercial society from collapsing under its internal, structural and sometimes ruinous dysfunctions.

We use now Figure 3.1, drawn for an economy of two people, A and B, two goods, Y (numeraire) and Q, and a negative consumption externality caused by Q, to provide intuitive explanations/interpretations of: (i) the two types of inefficiency associated with a non-externality-based price system in the presence of externalities, (ii) the efficiency conditions, and (iii) the sheer complexity of an ideal externality-based price system aimed at ensuring a gravitation towards efficiency, through *full internalization* of the externality.

(i) Consider point 1, with quantity Q_1 and price P_1. The figure shows neatly where the two types of inefficiency lie. One is the excessive total amount of Q. According to eq (10) efficiency is at point 3, with $Q^* < Q_1$, and the welfare loss is measured by the shaded area $1-3-4$. The other is the inefficient distribution of Q_1 among the two consumers. The distribution is q_{A1}, q_{B1}, but eq (10) tells us also that the SMB of the two consumers must be equal to each other, and points A_1 and B_1 show that they are not.

(ii) The two efficiency conditions of eq (10) are that total quantity must correspond to point 3, and its distribution among the consumers must correspond to points A^*, B^*.

(iii) Students of economics are often taught that if the consumption of Q causes a negative externality, then its price should move from point 1 to some higher point like 2, i.e. from price P_1 to some higher price like P_2, estimated to reflect the higher SMC due the externality. But this is not correct. In order to correct the externality a single price is not enough. The two consumers should face *two different prices*, P_A^*, P_B^*, so as to achieve not only the efficient total quantity Q^*, but also its efficient distribution q_A^*, q_B^* among the consumers. With a price increase to P_2 the total quantity would be okay

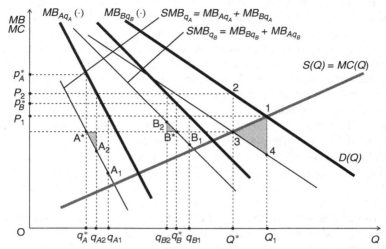

Figure 3.1 Consumption externalities: the efficient price system

(notice, however, that the optimal increase $P_1 \rightarrow P_2$ depends on a *combination* of the vertical distances between the curves $MB_{iq_i}(\cdot)$ and $SMB_{q_i}(\cdot)$ of the two consumers), but there would still be a welfare loss due to its wrong distribution q_{A2}, q_{B2}. As already seen the right distribution corresponds to points A^*, B^*, and the welfare loss of the wrong distribution is measured by the two shaded triangles around those points (in the figure here they are small, but in reality they could be quite large).

The graphic exercise of Figure 3.1 is very simple, but it is enough to prove that in the real world, quite apart from problems of market power and informational asymmetries, a price system capable of overcoming the welfare losses due to externalities would have to be a truly complex one, and in many cases its implementation would be practically impossible.

Production externalities: Social cost minimization under deterministic social damage

We want to investigate whether and to what extent it is possible to internalize negative environmental production externalities of a deterministic nature, defined in short as pollution of the environment (water, air, soil, atmosphere, biosphere, etc.) caused by the production activities of certain industries. The general idea is that when certain production activities cause pollution of some kind, their social cost consists of two components. One is the direct cost of producing the industries' output. The other is the additional damage imposed on people and/or other industries by reducing the welfare of the former and/or increasing the direct production costs of the latter. On the other hand, the direct cost of production activities causing pollution increases when pollution decreases, because decreasing pollution means cleaner and more expensive technologies and/or more and better purification and waste disposal facilities. As a consequence, the problem we face is one of *minimizing the total social cost* of producing the polluting industries' outputs. If pollution increases, their direct production costs decrease, but at the same time the damage/cost imposed on people and/or other industries increases. Essentially, internalizing the production externality of environmental pollution means bringing – as far as it is possible – these two opposite cost-affecting roles of pollution itself into the price system. The model that follows is a revision of Varian (1992: 432–8), aimed at a more effective highlighting of the nature and limitations of this particular type of internalization mechanism.

Assume there are n industries identified by the type of their output $q_i, i = 1, ..., n$, causing a negative externality like water pollution, or CO_2 emissions, or a similar deterministic environmental pollution, called pollution for short. Each polluting industry causes a certain amount of *individual pollution* x_i, whose sum $X = \sum_i x_i$ is the *total amount of pollution*.

Assume the affected community consists of m members (people and/or industries) identified as $a_k, k = 1, .., m$. Each polluting industry derives a benefit from its own pollution x_i, in the form of a reduced cost of production. For each industry i the cost of producing q_i is increasing in q_i and decreasing in x_i, because reducing x_i for any given level of output means using cleaner and more costly technologies or spending more on purification facilities. On the contrary, each member of the community suffers a certain damage caused to him by the *total* amount X of pollution. Total pollution can thus be viewed as a *public bad*, whose cost is the vertical sum of the *individual damages* suffered by each member of the affected community (in the case of public goods we talk of a total benefit equal to the vertical sum the individual benefits received). We formally represent the situation as follows.

First we define the cost structure of the polluting industries

$$c_i(q_i, x_i), i = 1, ...n : \text{cost of production of industry } i \qquad (11)$$

$$\sum_i x_i = X : \text{total pollution}$$

$$c'_{iq_i}(q_i, x_i) \equiv MC_{q_i}(\cdot) > 0 : \text{positive, and increasing over } q_i \forall x_i \qquad (12)$$

$$c'_{ix_i}(q_i, x_i) \equiv MC_{x_i}(\cdot) < 0 : \text{negative, and increasing over } x_i \forall q_i \qquad (13)$$

Then we define the damage to the community

$$c_k(X), k = 1,..m : \text{individual damage suffered from} \qquad (14)$$
$$\text{total pollution}$$

$$\sum_k c_x(X) : \text{total damage} \qquad (15)$$

$$c'_{kX}(X) \equiv MC_{kX}(\cdot) > 0 : \text{positive and increasing over } X \qquad (16)$$

We want to find the total amount of X and its inter-industry distribution (x_i) that minimize the *social cost* of producing whatever output vector (q_i) the industries choose to produce in their profit maximizing behaviour:

$$\min_{x_i} \sum_i c_i(q_i, x_i) + \sum_k c_k(X) = C(q_i, x_i) \qquad (17)$$

The *FOC* are given by

$$C'_{x_i}(\cdot) = 0$$

$$\rightarrow c'_{ix_i}(q_i, x_i) + \sum_k c'_{kX}(X) = 0 \qquad (18)$$

$$\rightarrow -MC_{ix_i}(\cdot) \equiv MB_{ix_i}(\cdot) = \sum_k MC_{kX}(\cdot)$$

Taking the output vector (q_i) as a parameter these are n eqs in the n variables (x_i). Under the usual convenient assumptions on the shape of the individual cost functions, they yield a unique solution vector of individual amounts of pollution as a function of the vector of individual outputs

$$x_i^*((q_i)) \rightarrow X^* = \sum_i x_i^*((q_i)) \qquad (19)$$

Substituting (19) into (17) yields the *minimized total social cost function*, as a function of the output vector (q_i)

$$\hat{C}(\cdot) = \sum_i c_i(q_i, x_i^*(\cdot)) + \sum_k c_k(X^*(\cdot)) = \hat{C}(q_i) \qquad (20)$$

For any output vector that may be chosen by the polluting industries in their profit maximizing behaviour, $\hat{C}(q_i)$ is the minimum social cost for producing it, obtained when the government chooses the optimal amount of pollution X^*, and a competitive market for pollution rights leads the polluting industries to choose the optimal inter-industry distribution (x_i^*) of that total amount.

Assuming two polluting industries, q_1, q_2, and two damaged people/industries, a_1, a_2, the solution to the model is represented graphically in Figure 3.2. On one side we have the polluting industries that benefit from their individual pollution. Each line $MB_{1_{x_1}}$ and $MB_{2_{x_2}}$ is the individual demand for X by the corresponding polluting industry, represented by the marginal benefit (marginal cost reduction) that it derives from its individual pollution x_i. Their *horizontal* summation, drawn as the *thick black line*, is the polluting industries' total demand for X. On the other side we have the people/industries that are damaged by total pollution. Each line MC_{1X} and MC_{2X} represents the individual marginal damage (cost) suffered from total X by the corresponding member of the affected community. Their *vertical* summation, drawn as the *thick grey line*, is the social marginal damage (cost) caused by X. Point 1 corresponds to the total amount of X that minimizes the social cost of producing any output vector (q_1, q_2) of the two industries. Points 2 and 3 correspond to the efficient inter-industry distribution (x_1^*, x_2^*) of the total efficient amount X^*, in the sense that if the efficient total X^* were distributed differently, then the total social cost of producing (q_1, q_2) would not be minimized, as the figure clearly shows. As for point $v_X^*(q_1, q_2)$, its interpretation is the well-known one in terms of an artificial market of pollution rights PR. A benevolent and perfectly informed government chooses the optimal total amount X^* and the corresponding total amount of PRs to be thrown into the market. Then a competitive market for the existing PRs would generate $v_X^*(q_1, q_2)$ as their clearing price, and (x_1^*, x_2^*) as their inter-industry distribution. Notice further that the figure shows intuitively the dependence of the solution from the output vector (q_1, q_2): clearly, in general, different output vectors (q_1, q_2) generate different MB lines, and thus different points 1, 2, 3.

This formal and graphic exercise, though abstract and highly stylized, illustrates in a straightforward manner an important theoretical and practical point concerning the possibility of internalizing production externalities, which we may summarize as follows. We know that the market cannot ensure the provision of public goods in a political community because the market rests on profit and competition and public goods do not directly generate profits. The provision of public goods requires cooperation. But at the level of a political community the

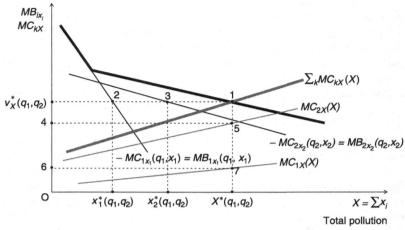

Figure 3.2 Internalizing deterministic production externalities

incentive to freely cooperate is weak or non-existent, while it is the incentive to free ride that dominates. The dominating status of the incentive to free ride implies that the only way to ensure the provision of public goods is through government enforced cooperation. Now, what holds for public goods holds also, mutatis mutandis, for public bads. As we have just seen, in the case of environmental production externalities the social damage caused by pollution, associated to total pollution X, and defined and measured as $\sum_k MC_{kX}$, has the nature of a *public bad*, while

the benefits derived from pollution, associated to the individual amount of pollution generated by the single agent, and defined and measured as $-MC_{ix_i} \equiv MB_{ix_i}$, have the nature of *private marketable gains*. It follows, in short, that only a partial internalization of this type of externality is possible. The internalizable part can be dealt with through the creation of a market for pollution rights. The non-internalizable part concerns three aspects, very neatly highlighted by the model. First, the market for pollution rights is an *artificial one* because although it is there potentially, it does not emerge by itself. In order to emerge it needs outside government intervention, consisting in the establishment by law that if an industry wants to pollute, it must *buy* a corresponding amount of *PR*, either from the government itself, or from other industries ready to supply them. Unlike this one, ordinary markets (such as the market for cars for instance) do not depend on such outside intervention in order to emerge. They emerge by themselves through the spontaneous meeting of buyers and sellers. In studying the operation of this type of market in practice, and in designing the appropriate public policy interventions, account must be taken of its artificial nature as a source of differences with respect to *natural* markets, with particular reference to what institutions and rules are needed to bring it close to competitive conditions. Second, the artificial market for pollution rights does not determine the efficient total amount of pollution. The amount can be determined in the abstract, in theory, but for the reasons given above its determination in practice must be made by the government, on the basis of all sorts of available technical and economic information. Third, ideally, but of course only ideally, the total revenue obtained from the sale of the *PRs*, equal to the area $v_X^* - 1 - X^* - O$ should then be divided among the damaged subjects – to compensate them for the damage suffered – into area $6 - 7 - X^* - O$ to individuals/industries a_1, and area $4 - 5 - X^* - O$ to individuals/industries a_2.

Social cost minimization under stochastic social damage

In this section we extend the analysis of the previous one to the case in which the productive activity of an industry or firm does not always cause with certainty a certain type of environmental pollution (such as CO_2 emissions or environment damaging waste disposal), but – due to its particular nature – it is liable to cause a damage to the environment accidentally, with a probability that is inversely related to the 'amount' of effort spent by the industry to prevent the accident. The model we describe preserves the simplicity and generality of the previous one, so that we may easily highlight what are the basic structural changes brought into picture when we move from a deterministic to a stochastic environmental social damage. In the subsequent sections we will discuss the special case of oil spills, and the problem of the optimal regulation of such stochastically polluting industries, on the basis of the more refined formulations of the present framework used in the current literature.

Consider an industry or firm producing some output, and suppose that its production activity carries a natural risk of accidents. It may accidentally cause an environmental damage, called pollution for short, as before. A typical case is that of oil multinationals using tanker ships for oil transportation, or operating offshore platforms, but there are innumerable other similar cases. If the accident occurs we may consider two types of damage: a private damage to the company, consisting in the loss of output or other revenue losses or cost increases due to the accident, and a social damage to the general community caused by the environmental pollution due to the accident. Both damages are stochastic in nature, and we represent this by applying to them a certain probability. Let us represent the *total social cost* function associated to the production activity of this particular company by the following eq

$$c(\cdot) = c(q) + p(z, \overline{p})\left[L(y,q) + D(q)\right] + y + z \tag{21}$$

$c(q)$ is the direct production cost of q. $L(y,q)$ is the private loss suffered by the company in case of accident. We assume that its size increases in general with the level of the company's activity/output q, and decreases with the level of *self-insurance* y. Self-insurance y stands for the provisions arranged by the company to reduce the severity of its own losses in case of accident, and we normalize their price to unity. $D(q)$ is the social damage caused by the accident, and we similarly assume that in general it increases in q. We denote the probability of the accident's occurrence by $p(z, \overline{p})$, where $\overline{p}$ stands for some level of positive *exogenous* probability, and z for the level of *self-protection*. Self-protection z stands for the provisions arranged by the company to reduce the probability of the accident's occurrence, and we also normalized their price to unity. $p(\cdot)$ increases in $\overline{p}$ and decreases in z.

We now want to find the pair (y, z) that minimizes the total social cost associated to whatever level q of productive activity is undertaken by this company. The (social) *FOC* of the problem are given by

$$c'_y(\cdot) = 0 \rightarrow -p(z, \overline{p})L'_y(y,q) = 1 \tag{22}$$

$$c'_z(\cdot) = 0 \rightarrow -p'_z(z, \overline{p})\left[L(y,q) + D(q)\right] = 1 \tag{23}$$

Taking $\overline{p}, q$ as parameters, these are two eqs in the two choice variables y, z. Under the usual convenient assumptions on the shape of the functions they yield a unique pair of social cost minimizing choice variables

$$y^*(\overline{p}, q) \tag{24}$$

$$z^*(\overline{p}, q)$$

But clearly this is not the company's profit maximizing market choice. In order to find it we simply remove the social damage $D(q)$ from (21). The resulting function is the total *private* cost function of the company

$$c(\cdot) = c(q) + p(z, \overline{p})L(y,q) + y + z \tag{25}$$

whose new minimizing (market) *FOC*

$$c'_y(\cdot) = 0 \rightarrow -p(z,\overline{p})L'_y(y,q) = 1 \tag{26}$$

$$c'_z(\cdot) = 0 \rightarrow -p'_z(z,\overline{p})L(y,q) = 1 \tag{27}$$

yield the new private cost minimizing choice variables

$$\hat{y}(\overline{p},q) \tag{28}$$
$$\hat{z}(\overline{p},q)$$

The differences between the private and social cost minimizing solutions can be easily explained and commented with the help of Figures 3.3 and 3.4.

In Figure 3.3 we graphically represent the private cost minimizing choice of y. It is obtained at point P_1 where the curve $-p(z,\overline{p})L'_y(y,q) = MB_y(z,\overline{p},y,q)$ in eq (26), which is the expected private marginal benefit derived from y represented as a function of y for any given values of $z,\overline{p},q$, intersects the marginal cost of y, equal to unity. We denote this privately optimal level of y by $\hat{y}(z,\overline{p},q)$. Since by our assumptions the accident's probability $p(z,\overline{p})$ is a decreasing function of the amount of self-protection effort z spent by the company, we can see in the figure that when z increases, the privately optimal level $\hat{y}$ decreases, because the expected marginal benefit curve of eq (26) shifts downwards. The intuition is of course that if the accident's probability diminishes, then also the expected benefit from a marginal increase in self-insurance diminishes.

In Figure 3.4 we graphically represent the private cost minimizing choice of z. It is obtained at point P_1 in the same way as y. The curve $-p'_z(z,\overline{p})L(y,q) = MB_z(z,\overline{p},y,q)$ in eq (27) is the expected private marginal benefit derived from z represented as a function of z for any given values of $\overline{p},y,q$, and it intersects the marginal cost of z, equal to unity, at the privately optimal level of z denoted by $\hat{z}(\overline{p},y,q)$. By construction, moving from the expected private to the expected social marginal benefit derived from z means moving to the upwards shifted curve $-p'_z(z,\overline{p})[L(y,q)+D(q)]$ of eq (23), whose intersection with the horizontal marginal cost line is at point P_2 to the right of P_1. We denote this socially optimal level of z by $z^*(\overline{p},y,q)$, with $z^*(\cdot) > \hat{z}(\cdot)$ being of course a fully intuitive result.

Using the above graphical analysis we may summarize the difference between private and social cost minimization by the following relations

$$\hat{y}(\overline{p},q) > y^*(\overline{p},q) \tag{29}$$

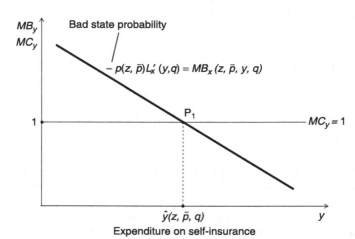

Figure 3.3 Internalizing stochastic production externalities: self-insurance

$$\hat{z}(\overline{p}, q) < z^*(\overline{p}, q)$$

Since $z^*(\cdot)$ must necessarily be higher than $\hat{z}(\cdot)$, as shown in Figure 3.4, this also implies that $y^*(\cdot)$ must be lower than $\hat{y}(\cdot)$, because $\hat{y}(\cdot)$ is a decreasing function of z, as shown in Figure 3.3. In words: the socially optimal level of a company's investment in self-protection is higher than the privately optimal level because account must be taken of the social damage, but the socially optimal level of its investment in self-insurance is lower than the socially optimal level, because with a higher self-protection the probability of an accident's occurrence is lower, and therefore also the expected private marginal benefit from self-insurance diminishes.

The analysis of this section, though very stylized and formally simple, is nevertheless sufficient to highlight two important differences between the instruments for internalizing environmental production externalities in the deterministic and the stochastic cases. In the deterministic case all industries causing a certain type of pollution can be brought together, the government must try to approximate as best as it can a socially optimal total amount of pollution, and then the rest of the job can be entrusted, at least in principle, to market mechanisms via the creation of an artificial market for pollution rights. In the stochastic case the analysis suggests that the externality must be dealt with at company, or at most at industry level, and that no market mechanisms of the pollution rights type can be devised. The only way to internalize pollution is to bring the stochastic social damage into the cost function of the particular company/industry

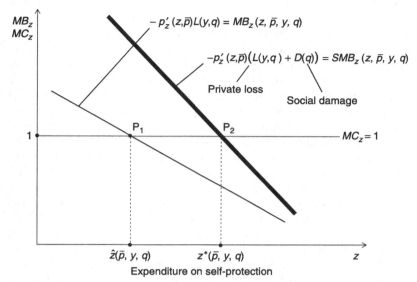

Figure 3.4 Internalizing stochastic production externalities: self-protection

under consideration, by converting it into a (stochastic) component of its cost of production, so that it would become profitable for the company/ industry to increase its investment in self-protection. The most immediate way to do this is of course to let it be known that in case of accident the company/industry will have to pay some compensating penalty proportional to the social damage. But incentives to increase investment in self-protection can also be created with more indirect measures, some of which are discussed in the following sections.

Stochastic externalities: an application to the economics of oil spills

When an event is stochastic there are two important properties that must be taken into account in our policy approach. First, when pollution is stochastic the polluted cannot associate pollution to the polluter action in a necessary way, and this constrains their ability to contract on pollution abatement or prevention activities. The departure from the hypothesis of determinism makes information asymmetries between polluter and polluted more likely. Victims may be constrained to contracts on realized damages or be forced to engage in expensive monitoring that may allow them to contract on the polluter activities contributing to pollution damages. Second, stochastic pollution problems mean that at least one agent involved in the Coasean bargain will have a stochastic income stream, suggesting a role for risk preferences (Coase 1960). Greenwood and Ingene (1978) found large heterogeneity in risk preferences across individuals, and, as noted by Cicchetti and Dubin (1994), risk-aversion varies systematically in a population, and varies with the level of income. Given wide variations in the wealth and size of the agents generating and suffering from pollution, agents are likely to differ in their ability and willingness to risk. These heterogeneous risk preferences will, of course, manifest themselves in equilibrium contracts. Macroeconomic models often use a representative agent framework, which does not capture, nor account for, such differences. Following the established literature (Hanley et al. 2007), risk can be defined by combining two distinct elements: the probability that a good or bad event may occur, and the outcomes or consequences following its actual occurrence. The aim of environmental policy is about changing both the probabilities and the outcomes, so that people may face a different, less risky environmental state of nature, the goal being less environmental risk at a lower cost. As emphasized in the older literature (Ehrlich and Becker 1972; Garen 1988; Shogren 1990; Shogren and Crocker 1991, 1994), environmental risk can be divided into two broad types: exogenous and endogenous. *Exogenous risk* means that a person takes the probabilities of good and bad states of nature as given and beyond his control (e.g. wind generated by a hurricane, the wind direction carrying pollution after an accident, the magnitude of an earthquake). In such cases the role of economics is to decide how to rank risky alternatives on the basis of the risk preferences across society, to evaluate costs and benefits of collective programmes aimed at reducing the outcomes' damage, and to develop institutions to pool and share risk across people and across good and bad states of the world (e.g. insurance markets). This world-view has dominated the modelling of choice under risk for the past two centuries. *Endogenous risk*, on the other hand, addresses the idea that individuals have some personal control over the set of probabilities and outcomes of the relevant states of the world. Personal attitudes towards risk and the available technologies to reduce risk might alter the risk faced. Following the traditional modelling approach, the individual choice framework changes when moving from an exogenous to an endogenous risk setting.

Exogenous and endogenous risk

There are states of the world that people cannot affect themselves through their private actions (e.g. you cannot control the probability that lightning will strike your house, this probability is exogenous to you). The theory of choice under risk as defined by the classic model is based on expected utility theory (EU) (von Neumann and Morgenstern 1947). This theory is based on the assumption that if preferences satisfy the four key axioms of completeness, transitivity, continuity, and independence the individual's behaviour can be modelled using the maximization of an expected utility function (see Mas-Colell et al. 1995: Chapter 6).

Suppose we have two states of the world, one good and the other bad. In the exogenous risk setting, we have

$$EU = pU(w - L) + (1 - p)U(w) \tag{30}$$

where w represent fixed exogenous wealth, L represent uncertain damages or losses[1] and p is the probability that the bad state of nature occurs.[2]

Common sense and everyday evidence demonstrate that human actions make environmental risks endogenous. We invest resources to change the chances that good things happen and bad things do not (Ehrlich and Becker 1972). Shibata and Winrich (1983) explored the endogeneity of the loss function by considering private actions undertaken by individuals that reduce the damages from pollution (a public bad). Thus, a person has preferences over outcomes and preferences over different states of nature that define those outcomes, and makes choices to secure the more preferred lotteries. Self-protection is investment made to reduce the probability of incurring any bad outcomes. Self-insurance investment consists of expenditures made to reduce loss caused by the occurrence of the unwanted event.

Consider a risk-averse person who must decide ex ante how to invest resources to control privately the risks she meets. Because of moral hazard, adverse selection, and non-independence of risks, this person cannot acquire enough market insurance to assure her ex ante utility level is maintained whether or not the harm occurs (Shogren and Crocker 1991).

Unlike the exogenous setting, the endogenous risk framework can be written as

$$EU = p(z, \overline{p})\, U(w - L(y) - y - z) + (1 - p(z, \overline{p}))U(w - y - z) \tag{31}$$

where as in the section on stochastic externalities, z is self-protection, y self-insurance, and $\overline{p}$ an exogenous uncontrollable probability, sometimes called background risk. As already indicated in eq (21), self-protection represents private investments to modify the probability that a good/bad state occurs; self-insurance are expenditures to reduce loss severity if the bad state occurs.

In the endogenous risk model, the probabilities of a good and bad state occurring are now written as functions of self-protection, z, and an exogenous probability, $\overline{p}$ (see Hanley et al. 2007: 401). Assume more self-protection reduces the chance of the bad state occurring:

$$p'_z(z,\overline{p}) < 0 \tag{32}$$

and greater exogenous probability increases the chance:

$$p'_{\overline{p}}(z,\overline{p}) > 0 \tag{33}$$

In addition, losses are a function of investments in self-insurance, y, so that $L' < 0$.

Assuming that the prices of self-protection and self-insurance are normalized to unity for simplicity, the optimality condition for self-protection (z) becomes:

$$\begin{aligned}
p'_z(\cdot)\big(U(w-L(y)-y-z)-U(w-y-z)\big) = \\
= p(\cdot)\big(U'(w-L(y)-y-z)\big)+(1-p(\cdot))(U'(w-y-z))
\end{aligned} \tag{34}$$

The left term is the marginal benefit of self-protection, defined by the decreased chance of the bad state weighted by the utility difference between the two states. The right term is the marginal cost.

The optimality condition for self-insurance y is:

$$\begin{aligned}
-p(\cdot)\big(U'(w-L(y)-y-z)(L'(y)+1) = \\
= (1-p(\cdot))(U'(w-y-z))
\end{aligned} \tag{35}$$

The left term is the marginal benefit of self-insurance as defined by the net reduction in loss, assuming $|L'(y)| > 1$ and the right term is the marginal cost. The key point here is the term $p'_z(z,\overline{p}) < 0$ because it provides curvature to the decision problem rather than just the curvature provided by assumptions of risk preferences based on the utility function. This introduces technology into risk reduction, and amplifies or decreases the preferences of risk reduction as implied by the utility function. Both technology and tastes matter here (Ehrlich and Becker 1972).

One can also write the expected utility model as uncertainty over a continuous set of states of the world (see Hanley et al. 2007: 401). Now considering the continuous case, the person ex ante selects z and y to maximize his van Neumann–Morgenstern utility index:

$$EU = \int_0^{\bar{x}} U(w - L(y,x) - c(y,z))dF(\bar{x}, \alpha, z) \tag{36}$$

where w is endowed income, $L(y,x)$ is the money equivalent of realized damage severity from hazard exposure, and x is, here, a non-negative random variable, indicating the accident severity, which could be the spill severity, for example an oil spill in the habitat of a species in danger of extinction. The accident severity ranges from 0, that means no accident occurs, to $\bar{x}$, the upper bound, and follows a probability distribution, $x \sim F(x,z,\alpha): X \rightarrow [0,1]$. It is worth noting that self-protection, representing private investment to increase the probability that a good state occurs, affects the probability of an accident while self-insurance, representing expenditure to reduce the severity of the bad state if it is realized, only affects severity when the accident does occur. $c(y,z)$ is the cost function for self-care and α is an index of exogenous riskiness.

Optimal regulation of a stochastically polluting industry

Since many environmental accidents do not always occur in a well-regulated environment, we want to analyse the possibility of adapting deterministic environmental policies to uncertain contexts in such recognizable forms.

As stated by Shavell (1979), the principal–agent literature provides a convenient framework to analyse the problem of regulating a firm that causes random accidents such as oil spills. The standard concept of strict liability can be seen as a principal–agent contract that depends only on the outcome. Following Cohen (1987), the principal is assumed to be a government with regulatory authority over firms and the agent is a firm that stochastically pollutes the environment. The problem is to find a penalty function that determines the amount that the polluter firm must pay to the government so that the firm's objective function coincides with the principal's expected utility function when the government is assumed to be a social welfare maximizer.

Rearranging the model of Cohen (1987) according to the setting introduced in the previous section, we obtain the following expected profit of the firm

$$EU = \int_0^{\bar{x}} U(L(y,x) - P(x)T(x,z))dF(x,z,\alpha) - y - z \tag{37}$$

where $P(x)$ is the probability of being detected by the authority and $T(x,z)$ is the penalty imposed by the government once the externality is generated and the firm is detected.[3] The cost function for self-care, $c(y,z)$, is supposed to be linear in y and z.

The principal's expected utility function may be written as

$$EW = \int_0^{\bar{x}} \left\{ D[(1-r)x] + C(rx) + L(y,x) \right\} dF(x;z,\alpha) - y - z \tag{38}$$

where $D[(1-r)x]$ is the environmental damage, $C(rx)$ are the cleanup costs. r is chosen by the government so that given a pollution amount x, $(1-r)x$ may remain in the environment and rx must be cleaned up.

The regulator will choose the required levels of self-protection and self-insurance that maximize eq (38). Since eq (38) is a Riemann–Stieltjes integral, a generalization of the Riemann integral, it can be rewritten as

$$EW = \int_0^{\bar{x}} \left\{ D[(1-r)x] + C(rx) + L(y,x) \right\} f(x;z,\alpha)dx - z - y \tag{39}$$

The first order condition with respect to z is

$$\int_0^{\bar{x}} \left\{ D[(1-r)x] + C(rx) + L(y,x) \right\} f_z(x;z,\alpha)dx = 1 \tag{40}$$

that is, the optimal self-protection choice is derived by equating the social marginal benefit associated with an additional increase of self-protection with its marginal cost (assumed to be unity).

The first order condition with respect to y is

$$\int_0^{\bar{x}} L_y(y,x) \left\{ D[(1-r)x] + C(rx) + L(y,x) \right\} f(x;z,\alpha)dx = 1 \tag{41}$$

As in the above simpler model with two states of nature developed by Hanley et al. (2007), we assume $|L_y'(y,x)| > 1$ and $L_y'(y,x) < 0$ so that the agent equates the marginal cost of influencing the severity of oil spill with the marginal wealth gained.

As the amount of information available to the environmental regulator is limited and this cannot directly control the level of self-protection and self-insurance performed by the oil company, the principal has to design a penalty whereby the firm is induced to adopt the socially optimal level of self-protection and self-insurance. Following the Cohen (1987) framework, the penalty can be designed as

$$T(x,z) = \frac{D[(1-r)x] + C(rx)}{P(x)} \tag{42}$$

The optimal penalty function depends directly on the social damage that remains in the environment plus the cleanup costs and inversely on the probability of being detected. This is just Becker's optimal penalty which is equal to the ratio between the harm and the probability of detection, which induces firms to adopt the socially optimal level of effort (Becker 1968). If the oil company is made responsible for cleanup costs and for any residual damage, the optimal level of cleanup will be chosen by equating marginal cleanup costs to marginal damages (Polinsky and Shavell 1994).

Substituting (42) into the expected profit of the oil company (37), we simply obtain (38).[4] In Cohen's model the penalty is a strict-liability standard because the polluter is punished regardless of its level of self-protection and self-insurance. As pointed out by Posner (1977), strict liability is generally preferred to a negligence standard because it opens room for technological improvements allowing for a decrease in the size and probability of pollution.

Several issues arise when dealing with the above penalty function. On one hand, as noted by Van't Veld et al. (1997), the penalty as expressed in eq (42) may present an upper bound. High penalties might not always be practical because of the limited ability of the firms to pay. This is the judgement-proof problem addressed by Shavell (1986), Beard (1990), Polborn (1998), and Innes (1999a). On the other hand, since $T(x,z)$ is a linear combination of the random variable x, (42) is the equation of a stochastic penalty which is distributed following the probability distribution, $T(x,z) \sim F(x,z,\alpha)$. This result contrasts with the fact that the penalty (tax) should be certain.

The issue of finding a stochastic penalty function is partially overcome in the endogenous risk framework presented by Sproul and Zilberman (2011). The authors examined the regulation of stochastic externalities in which the problem of oil spills can be straightforwardly addressed. This paper, based on a principal–agent model with moral hazard like Cohen's model, introduces a conceptual framework for regulating an industry of risk-neutral and stochastically polluting firms. It develops a general model allowing for information asymmetry, prevention, and cleanup actions (both ex ante and ex post), and for the exact prevention mechanism to affect the probability and/or severity of oil spill accidents.

The 'holy trinity' of environmental economic policy, as the authors call Pigouvian taxes, abatement subsidies, and systems of tradable pollution permits (TPPs), and described in Baumol and Oates (1988), must be revised taking into account the uncertainty adjusted version of tax and subsidy policies. While all of these policies can achieve optimal levels of pollution, the difference lies in the allocation of resources; taxes take money out of the polluting industry, subsidies transfer money in, and tradable permits keep all the money within the industry, but shift funds from dirtier to cleaner firms in equilibrium. Moreover, the authors demonstrate that uncertainty may exacerbate discrepancies between resource allocations when compared to the deterministic setting.

Following the setup showed in the previous paragraphs, we illustrate the general framework of decision-making under uncertainty as shown by Sproul and Zilberman (2011). Compared to Cohen, they complicate the model by considering the decisions of an individual agent with riskiness of type α. The agents can be differentiated by type, which is a feature representing the inherent riskiness of their actions. Their model allows one to distinguish, for example, between oil companies operating onshore instead of offshore drilling. The regulator cannot observe the agents' type or an accident's severity, but both parties are aware of any damages, which are supposed to be measurable and traceable to their source.

Instead of obtaining a penalty function, Sproul and Zilberman (2011) consider an agent (firm) maximizing an objective function in which the social damage $D(x)$ is included. The agent, behaving optimally, faces the following objective function:

$$E[\pi] = w - z - \int_0^{\bar{x}} (L(x) + D(x) + c(x)) dF(x, z, \alpha) \tag{43}$$

In this setting, z is planned to be self-protection (lower probability of accident occurring) and/or self-insurance (decreased severity if an accident does occur). They assume that $F_z' \geq 0$ $\forall x$ and strictly greater for some x. Correspondingly, they suppose that $F_\alpha' \geq 0$ $\forall x$ and strictly lower for some x, in the sense of first-order stochastic dominance.

They also assume that prevention exhibits decreasing marginal returns because generally prevention expenditure is initially low, $F_{zz} \leq 0$ $\forall x$.

Using a backwards inductive approach, the authors solve first the optimal cleanup response for every outcome if the accident occurs and then this information is used to solve the choice for the ex ante care.

The unregulated case

The optimal level of z^* is compared with the level of self-care achieved with the unregulated case. Ignoring any utility payoff from doing the right thing, the oil companies will choose suboptimally if they are not responsible for releasing oil spills. Thus, the unregulated oil companies solve the following problem

$$\underset{z}{Max}\, E\left[\pi^{UR}\right] = w - z - \int_0^{\bar{x}} L(x)dF(x,z,\alpha) \qquad (44)$$

As in the optimal case a positive level of prevention effort is due to some personal loss that the agent faces when the accident occurs. In the absence of regulation the level of z is less than the optimal level. For a given riskiness type α, they obtain

$$\int_0^{\bar{x}}(F_z(z_{UR}^*)L_x')dx > \int_0^{\bar{x}}(F_z(z^*)L_x')dx \qquad (45)$$

Since $F_{zz} \leq 0$ $\forall x$ and strictly less than zero for some x, it follows that $z^* > z_{UR}^*$ (see Sproul and Zilberman 2011). They demonstrate that in order to protect their own losses firms choose some prevention care but its level is lower than the optimal level because oil companies disregard social accident costs

Tax policy (strict liability)

Tax policy under uncertainty can maximize social welfare similarly by forcing polluters to internalize the externality, that is, they will account for the social cost of their actions as part of their decision-making process. In fact, this is what happens when agents behave optimally (43). The main element of stochastic pollution taxes is that the tax amount cannot be fixed in advance because the optimal containment response is state-dependent, which would lead to second-best outcomes. Therefore, tax policy must take the form of strict liability and it will lead to socially optimal behaviour by making agents legally responsible to pay damages after a disaster, entirely aligning their personal incentives with the social objective. The responsibility system must rely on perfect revelation and traceability of social damages by regulators or by the individuals affected, and transaction costs of enforcement must be zero.

In this framework the main constraint in policy formation is represented by the agent's inability to pay. High penalties may not always be practical because oil companies may state bankruptcy and this constitutes an effective upper bound on financial penalties.[5] To overcome the above constraint, the authors suggest alternative policies to induce optimal producer behaviour.

Abatement subsidies

Subsidy programmes may achieve socially optimal outcomes, but their design must essentially differ from their deterministic counterpart. In a stochastic environment, the optimal behaviour is state-dependent, so the ex ante care investment is important, but it is not sufficient for an optimal outcome. As pointed out by Sproul and Zilberman (2011), in the stochastic setup two main issues arise: first, there is a budget constraint problem because ex ante care reduces the probability that an accident occurs, so that each agent should be paid in every period (even if no accident occurs). This solution can require enormous accessibility to financial resources. Second, in order to avoid perverse incentives the subsidy must be based on abatement below a fixed threshold and not proportional to the actual value of the damage. The grant cannot pay reimbursement for actual abatement of damages because rewarding agents may induce risky behaviour. A further issue in developing an optimal subsidy policy is finding a participation constraint inducing all agents to participate in the subsidy programme. Note that in some states of nature subsidy payments may also be negative. Therefore the difference between subsidy and tax policy consists only in the fact that subsidy programmes induce voluntary participation from polluter agents. To ensure that all agents play a voluntary part in the subsidy programme, the expected profits with no regulation must not exceed the expected profits generated by participation in the subsidy programme for all types of agents:

$$E[\pi^S] \geq E[\pi^{UR}] \qquad \forall \alpha \tag{46}$$

Thus, the subsidy programme requires more information than strict liability, and the regulator needs information about how profits might change when switching from an unregulated to a regulated environment. Specifically, the regulator needs to know the total externalities cost for the highest cost type, which may be the riskiest type. Paying subsidies in every period and for the most costly type in order to include all agents in the programme means that outliers in the distribution of agents may drive up the volume of subsidy payments to the polluting industry. In other words, while a strict liability system may face ability to pay constraints by polluters, the subsidy policy may face budget constraints by the government.

To conclude the analysis, the authors focus on a mutual insurance policy that is budget-neutral because it retains all funds within the polluting industry.

Mutual insurance

This third tool of environmental policy, proposed by Sproul and Zilberman (2011), has the flavour of a system of tradable permits. The idea is a mutual insurance for the polluter imposed by the regulator. Thus, no participating constraints must be satisfied, and the regulator enforces compulsory participation because there is no incentive from outside funds.

The insurance policy is funded by the companies themselves: agents with higher costs of pollution abatement subsidize those who are more efficient in provisions of pollution control. The resource allocation is similar to that of cap and trade policies in the deterministic environment: dirtier firms subsidize cleaner ones, defined according to the industry average.

Concluding remarks

The analysis of this chapter is based on the difference between the instruments for internalizing environmental production externalities of a deterministic or stochastic nature. In the case of deterministic externalities all industries causing a certain type of pollution are taken together, the government chooses some socially optimal or acceptable total amount of pollution, and then social cost minimization is pursued through artificial market mechanisms of pollution permits. In the case of stochastic externalities no market mechanism of the pollution permits type can be applied, and social cost minimization must be pursued at company, or at most at industry level. The element of uncertainty inherent in environmental accidents, such as oil spills and many others, has important implications for the design of environmental policy.

The chapter highlights the theoretical thread linking the literature on stochastic externalities in general and on oil spills in particular. We show that different authors at different times used the same theoretical framework for the optimal regulation of an industry of stochastically polluting risk neutral companies. The framework, which allows for informational asymmetry, prevention, and cleanup actions (both ex ante and ex post), and a mechanism to affect the accidents' probability and severity, shows that the only way to internalize stochastic pollution is to bring the stochastic social damage into the cost function of the particular company/industry under consideration, by converting it into a (stochastic) component of its cost of production, so as to make it profitable for the company/industry to increase its investment in self-protection.

Cohen's work (1987) focused on finding a stochastic penalty function capable of aligning company incentives to those of a social welfare maximizing regulator. Sproul and Zilberman (2011) identify three different policy regimes which satisfy, in a stochastic scenario, the role of their deterministic counterparts, showing that only a strict liability regime can generate sufficient funds to compensate for the social damage caused by environmental accidents. Such a regime would, however, be greatly limited by equity considerations and ability to pay constraints. The limitations can be overcome by subsidy programmes, which are in turn constrained by the regulator's ability to pay. The impossibility of identifying high-risk outliers and the accidents' rarity increase insurance premiums and compensation franchises. Abatement subsidies do not provide compensation to outside victims. Mutual insurance policies retain all funds in the industry without any mechanism for compensating outside victims, but have the advantage of being budget-neutral in expected value and of encouraging the transfer of resources from riskier to safer companies. The further advantage of the new risk-pooling scheme proposed by Sproul and Zilberman is that it simultaneously increases resource efficiency and minimizes resource redistribution.

Notes

1 Examples of these costs include the value of oil lost in an oil spill.
2 Here the analysis is conducted for each level q of productive activity undertaken by the company.
3 With respect to the model introduced by Cohen (1987), here we do not consider the level of government resources devoted to ex ante monitoring, those dedicated to detection, or the resources devoted to ex post monitoring of the firm's level of effort (self-protection and self-insurance). The same results are reached even without taking into account these parameters.

4 It is worth noting that in specifying the penalty function the government must also choose the optimal level of recovery rate r by equating marginal damage to marginal cleanup costs.
5 This is the judgement-proof problem addressed by Shavell (1986), Innes (1999a) and others.

References

Baumol, W. J. and Oates, W. E. 1988. *The Theory of Environmental Policy*, 2nd edition. New York: Cambridge University Press.

Beard, T. R. 1990. 'Bankruptcy and Care Choice'. *Rand Journal of Economics*, 21(4): 626–34.

Becker, G. S. 1968. 'Crime and Punishment: An Economic Approach'. *Journal of Political Economy*, 76: 169–217.

Cicchetti, C. J. and Dubin, J. A. 1994. 'A Microeconometric Analysis of Risk Aversion and the Decision to Self-Insure'. *Journal of Political Economy*, 102(1): 169–86.

Coase, R. H. 1960. 'The Problem of Social Cost'. *Journal of Law and Economics*, 3: 1–44.

Cohen, M. A. 1987. 'Optimal Enforcement Strategy to Prevent Oil Spills: An Application of a Principal–Agent Model with Moral Hazard'. *Journal of Law and Economics*, 30(1): 23–51.

Ehrlich, I. and Becker, G. S. 1972. 'Market Insurance, Self-Insurance, and Self-Protection'. *Journal of Political Economy*, 80: 623–48.

Garen, J. 1988. 'Compensating Wage Differentials and the Endogeneity of Job Riskiness'. *Review of Economics and Statistics*, 70(1): 9–16.

Greenwood, P. and Ingene, C. 1978. 'Uncertain Externalities, Liability Rules, and Resource Allocation'. *American Economic Review*, 68: 300–10.

Hanley, N., Shogren, J. and White, B. 2007. *Environmental Economics in Theory and Practice*, 2nd edition. New York: Palgrave Macmillan.

Innes, R. 1999a. 'Optimal Liability with Stochastic Harms, Judgement-Proof Injurers, and Asymmetric Information'. *International Review of Law and Economics*, 19: 181–203.

Innes, R. 1999b. 'Self-Policing and Optimal Law Enforcement when Violator Remediation is Valuable'. *Journal of Political Economy*, 107: 1305–25.

Mas-Colell, A., Whinston, M. and Green, J. 1995. *Microeconomic Theory*. Oxford: Oxford University Press.

Polborn, M. K. 1998. 'Mandatory Insurance and the Judgment-Proof Problem'. *International Review of Law and Economics*, 18(2): 141–6.

Polinsky, A. M. and Shavell, S. 1994. 'A Note on Optimal Cleanup and Liability After Environmentally Harmful Discharges'. *Research in Law and Economics*, 16: 17–24.

Posner, R. A. 1977. *Economic Analysis of Law*, 2nd edition. Boston: Little, Brown.

Shavell, S. 1979. 'Risk Sharing and Incentives in the Principal and Agent Relationship'. *Bell Journal of Economics*, 10: 55–73.

Shavell, S. 1986. 'The Judgment Proof Problem'. *International Review of Law and Economics*, 6: 45–58.

Shibata, H. and Winrich, J. S. 1983. 'Control of Pollution When the Offended Defend Themselves'. *Economica*, 50: 425–38.

Shogren, J. F. 1990. 'The Impact of Self-Protection and Self-Insurance on Individual Response to Risk'. *Journal of Risk and Uncertainty*, 3: 191–204.

Shogren, J. F. and Crocker, T. D. 1991. 'Risk, Self-Protection, and Ex Ante Economic Value'. *Journal of Environmental Economics and Management*, 20: 1–15.

Shogren, J. F. and Crocker, T. D. 1994. 'Rational Risk Valuation Given Sequential Reduction Opportunities'. *Economic Letters*, 44: 241–8.

Sproul, T. and Zilberman, D. 2011. 'Accidents Happen: The Effect of Uncertainty on Environmental Policy Design'. Agricultural and Applied Economics Association, Annual Meeting, 24–26 July, Pittsburgh, Pennsylvania (No. 103927).

Van't Veld, K., Rausser, G. and Simon, L. 1997. 'The Judgment Proof Opportunity'. *FEEM Nota di Lavoro*, 83.

Varian, H. 1992. *Microeconomic Analysis*, 3rd edition. New York: Norton.

von Neumann, J. and Morgenstern, O. 1947. *Theory of Games and Economic Behavior*. Princeton: Princeton University Press.

4 Environmental protection and the Green Paradox

State of the art and open issues

Laura Castellucci

Introduction

In 1975 the first textbook on environmental policy was published. At its start one reads:

> When the 'environmental revolution' arrived in the 1960s, economists were ready and waiting. The economic literature contained an apparently coherent view of the nature of the pollution problem together with a compelling set of implications for public policy. In short, economists saw the problem of environmental degradation as one in which economic agents imposed external costs upon society at large in the form of pollution. With no 'price' to provide the proper incentives for reduction of polluting activities, the inevitable result was excessive demands on the assimilative capacity of the environment. The obvious solution to the problem was to place an appropriate 'price', in this case a tax, on polluting activities so as to internalize the social costs. Marshall and Pigou had suggested such measures many decades earlier. Moreover, pollution and its control through so-called Pigouvian taxes had become a standard textbook case of the application of the principles of microeconomic theory. *Economists were thus ready to provide counsel to policy makers on the design of environmental policy.* However, things have proved not quite so simple as this.
>
> (Baumol and Oates 1988: 1)

Then in 1989 another book appeared (Pearce 1989), just two years after the release of the Brundtland Report (United Nations 1987), originally prepared as a report for the UK Department of the Environment on the meaning of the term 'sustainable development' therein put forward, but also addressing such issues as 'valuing the environment' and 'marked-based instruments'. Back then a consensus was found on the meaning of the term sustainable development as one that 'meets the needs of the present without compromising the ability of future generations to meet their own needs', and translates in non-declining human welfare over time. Since then many other similar reports/studies have been published which, together with an abundance of research papers addressing specific problems, would make the global village aware of both environmental problems and their possible solutions.

The 'environmental revolution' of the 1960s faded away leaving all externalities unaddressed and sustainable development an empty box for politicians who nowadays like to frequently resort to green washing. Fifty years on, notwithstanding further progress made by economists in their understanding of the interactions between the environment and the economy, the problems we face are qualitatively the same as those mentioned in the first textbook and blueprint, but quantitatively much worse if only for the demographical pressure. In 1960 less than 3 billion people were living on our planet while now they are more than 7 billion. Governments have been tinkering with the environmental tools for enacting environmental policies, but in no country does the environment appear to have top priority. Not surprisingly, progress in international agreements among countries has been very limited and so are the achievements in terms of alleviating environmental problems. Although during this period a few virtuous countries did unilaterally introduce some environmental corrections and also a few international treaties tried to do the same, with few exceptions results have been unnoticeable. This is the case with the greatest problem of them all: climate change. Moreover, following a recent approach which emerged from a debate first started by Sinn (2008, 2012a), environmental policies designed to curb emissions may actually backfire. This fact is known in the literature as the *Green Paradox* (GP).

The Green Paradox

We face a *Green Paradox* when well-meaning but imperfectly designed environmental policies to mitigate carbon emissions do in fact increase them. In the words of its initiator, Sinn:

> Resource owners aren't stupid ... The mere announcement of intentions to fight global warming made the world warm even faster. That is the Green Paradox. What the resource owners heard sounded to them like saber-rattling by people who planned to destroy their markets, or like an announced expropriation of their fossil-fuel deposits. They reacted the same way they deal with the risk

of expropriation by rivals who threaten to seize power and reallo-
cate the property rights: by speeding up extraction.

(2012a: 188–9)

And the speeding up of the extraction process increases CO_2 emissions.
This result, known as *intertemporal carbon leakage*, may appear only if
resource owners have enough time to respond to the demand-reducing
environmental policy by adjusting their supply. But if they do have time
to adjust their supply, the stricter they expect the policy to become, the
greater will be the quantities extracted earlier rather than later. Moreover,
Sinn points to the fact that when a country, or even a group of countries, *unilaterally* introduces an environmental policy to curb emissions,
as in the case of the EU, which started the emissions trading system
(ETS) in 2005, the total amount of emissions remains unaffected. This
discouraging result is due to the fact that the countries which do not
implement any emissions-reducing policies will actually replace the CO_2
not emitted by the green countries. According to the figures of CO_2
emissions produced by the International Energy Agency and reported in
Figure 4.1, this seems to be the case. The total amount of CO_2 has been
increasing since the early 1970s and no reduction has been generated by
the EU ETS. 'The EU's efforts to curb its carbon consumption didn't
even produce a kink in the curve depicting the relentlessly growing trend
of worldwide CO_2 emissions. Carbon leakage means that the carbon not
consumed in one country is instead consumed in another country' (Sinn
2012a: 129). Here we face a different type of carbon leakage, the one
among countries, known as *spatial leakage*.[1] The two types of leakage,
intertemporal and spatial, make up the Green Paradox. On one hand,
there are incentives to anticipate extraction and therefore changes in
the quantities extracted in each period tilt towards the present; on the
other, brown countries will replace green countries in the consumption
of CO_2. What we need now is an inquiry into the literature to look for
conditions causing more extraction in the present, or, in other words, to
discuss conditions under which different instruments of environmental
policy, from Pigouvian taxes to ETS to subsidies, do backfire so that
CO_2 emissions increase after their introduction.

The central point in the GP is that so far, attempts to introduce any
kind of environmental policies have been aimed at curbing fossil fuel
consumption, with complete disregard for the supply side of the market.
This is in fact the case with the EU. EU energy policy is characterized
by efforts to increase energy saving and efficiency, for example through
strict standards on the energy efficiency of buildings, which represent
40 per cent of the Union's final energy consumption,[2] or through

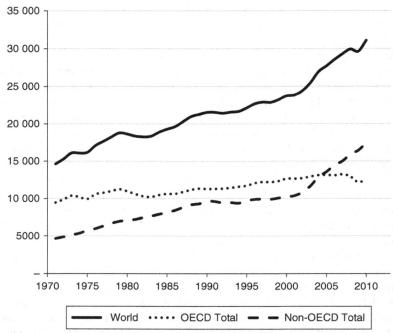

Figure 4.1 CO_2 emissions, million tonnes (reference approach)
Source: IEA (2012).

promotion of alternative clean sources for energy production, in place of dirty fossil fuels (EC Directive 2009, amending and subsequently repealing EC Directives 2001/77/EC and 2003/30/EC). And much in the same line, the EU transportation policy imposes emission controls in cars and quality requirements on fuel, gasoline and diesel (EC Directive 1998/70/EC, amended by EC Directive 2003/17/EC). When a successful demand-reducing policy causes the demand for energy to decline, will the resources' owners, oil sheikhs and gas oligarchs, continue to extract their resources at the same pace as in the absence of the policy? Or will they react by extracting less or more quantities? Or will they react by reducing the market resource price in order to capture an extra demand? Sinn and the followers of the GP believe that 'the reduction in demand will then simply lead to a lowering of fossil fuel prices' by increasing quantities extracted. In other words, demand-reducing policies affect the supply side of the market producing the unpleasant result of more CO_2 emissions by 'inducing firms and households in other parts of the world to consume the carbon that the "green" countries set free' (Sinn 2012b). We now briefly highlight the basic theory underlying the GP claim, leaving empirical evidence and discussion for the following section.

The basis for the GP is a standard exhaustible resource Hotelling model (Hotelling 1931). Within such a model Sinn (2008) analyses the effects of the introduction of two different types of taxes aimed at reducing demand, a cash flow tax and a sales tax, under the two alternative hypotheses of constancy or increase. Thus there are four scenarios in which to verify policy effectiveness in mitigating emissions and therefore climate change. The basic assumptions concern the stock of fossil fuel, assumed to be given, with extraction costs assumed to be stock-dependent, and the fact that no backstop technology enters the picture. For the existence of the GP the first (stock is given) and third (absence of alternative source) assumptions are necessary. In fact in a basic Hotelling model the optimal extraction path of a given resource stock subject to depletion in a certain number of years, says that the rate of return to the producer must grow at a rate equal to the rate of interest. Along the optimal path the resource owner is indifferent between investing in the extraction activity or in the financial market. The absence of an alternative source guarantees that the exhaustion of the resource follows the optimal path. These assumptions have been questioned on the grounds of lack of realism, in the sense that there are usually exploration activities under way. Since fossil fuels are simply stored under the earth crust and the ocean, to look for new reserves is the common situation, not an exceptional one. Analogously, technical progress is also always under way, and therefore present and potential backstop technologies[3] cannot be disregarded. Intuitively, if they are not disregarded it is possible that the resource stock will not be exhausted, in which case the GP would not occur. Researchers have integrated the Sinn model (2008) with both backstop technologies and exploration activities, and have deepened and enlarged his analysis to include a different climate policy instrument from the tax, such as a subsidy to new clean sources of energy to accelerate the substitution of oil. Most of the merit goes to the models by Hoel (2010, 2011), Gerlagh (2011), Smulders et al. (2010), Van der Ploeg and Withagen (2010, 2013) and Van der Ploeg (2013).

Interestingly enough, when considering additional features the GP appears to be less likely in general and to vanish altogether in some cases, as we will see. Moreover a distinction has been made in the literature between a Weak Green Paradox and a Strong Green Paradox, Gerlagh being the main contributor. The distinction between a weak and a strong paradox is not just a question of producing more precise definitions, because it has relevant theoretical and therefore policy implications. The two types of GP coincide with a short- and a long-run view of the policy impact respectively, and it is therefore intuitive to expect that the occurrence of the weak paradox does not necessarily imply the occurrence of the strong one. To provide insight into the two concepts we follow Gerlagh (2011). First it is necessary to define what we mean by climate change damage when greenhouse gas emissions are assumed proportional to the supply of depletable resources, and then to add that within the logic of the Green Paradox a delay in emissions is preferred to them occurring earlier. In a simple Hotelling model with constant extraction costs, competitive conditions, resource owners maximizing the net present value of supply, and the standard assumption of a more costly backstop technology (and corresponding choke price for the demand), the rent component of the price grows at an exponential pace equal to the interest rate. Using a shadow price on emissions, their net present value gives the climate change damage increasing at the pace of the rate of interest. The assumption concerning the preference for delayed emissions translates here into the assumption that the marginal damage increases at less than the rate of interest. Within this framework Gerlagh defines a *Weak Green Paradox* as the one occurring when an improvement in the backstop technology raises emissions in the short run because the resource owner anticipates extraction for fear of losing customers in the future to the competition of cleaner resources,[4] while a *Strong Green Paradox* occurs when the net present value of damage increases. The increase or decrease in the aggregate net present value of damage may be thought of as a measure of the change in 'green welfare'.

Gerlagh (2011) first addresses the fundamental question of having a scientific assessment of the quantity of fossil fuels we can continue to burn without risking an irreversible climate change, and then focuses on the effect of the introduction of a subsidy to new clean technologies as an alternative policy instrument to the tax for reducing emissions. Incidentally carbon taxes are commonly opposed on the basis of the competitiveness argument, which suggests that when a country introduces such a tax, production costs of the domestic firms increase causing their market share to shrink. Obviously no such type of argument applies to a subsidy, and although this is not a fault-free instrument, it may reduce emissions by accelerating transition to cleaner sources. Gerlagh begins by showing that, within the framework of an initial very simple Hotelling model and under certain precise conditions, both the weak and the strong paradox may occur. Things change in more sophisticated models such as his Models 2 and 3. Model 2 relaxes the fixed resource stock assumption and includes a perfect backstop technology in combination with increasing extraction costs with cumulative resource extraction. In Model 3 Gerlagh concentrates on the cost of the backstop technology and on the fact that there are several renewable (clean) energy sources, and no one is a perfect substitute for oil and other fossil fuels. Results from Model 2 show the existence of the weak paradox and the non-existence of the strong one. The intuitive reason for this is to be found in the fact that the net present value of damages stemming from the fossil fuel use is reduced as a consequence of the cheaper backstop that shortens the economic lifetime of oil. (Gerlagh calls attention to the substantial difference between Models 1 and 2 in that the physical exhaustion of fossil fuel of the first model is replaced by its economic exhaustion in the second one: the associated CO_2 emissions are therefore less, since an amount of oil is now left unextracted.) Results from Model 3 show that neither the weak paradox nor the strong one arises. Here the setting is more complex, but the intuition is that thanks to the cheaper substitutes the net present value of the rent falls as does the termination time, preventing both paradoxes from occurring (Gerlagh 2011).

Concerns about the existence of a Green Paradox, weak or strong, have given rise to a growing number of studies whose findings are in general in the direction of weakening the GP. Among such studies an interesting recent one (Fischer and Salant 2012) adds new findings and considerations in the debate by deepening the analysis of the intertemporal leakage when five types of fossil fuel are considered and four alternative policies enter the picture. The study may help in designing policy interventions tailored to the circumstances, because the four policy options – taxing emissions, improving energy efficiency, accelerating cost reductions in clean backstop technologies, and clean fuel blend mandate – may be ranked according to their capacity of delaying or anticipating emissions. Moreover there are two other reasons for giving due consideration to this paper's results. First, it emerges as a general result that when a policy becomes more stringent the intertemporal leakage rates decline. The result is important because it may be interpreted to support the introduction of a rather bold policy, as opposed to the current mild attempts by governments to adopt one, which reveal an unconvinced attitude towards the necessity of taking action now. Second, it calls attention to the importance of considering that different types of fossil fuels differ not only in terms of production costs but also in terms of quantifiable CO_2 emissions. It is a fact that, while soon after the industrial revolution the evolution in the use of fuel sources moved from the dirtiest to the cleanest ones (from coal to oil to gas), nowadays this trend is no more, and the newcomers, the so-called unconventional oils, are the dirtiest. This means that the type of fossil fuel burned is as important as the quantity burned, and if it is fully reasonable to expect the burning to follow the unit cost of production, commencing with the lowest costs source (Herfindahl 1967), the ordering in terms of emissions may differ from the ordering in terms of production costs. Leaving things to the market may be risky while a clean fuel blend mandate may be desirable, and as Fischer and Salant (2012) show, the policy seems to be effective.

Discussion and empirical evidence

One of the main problems in combating global warming is the substitutability among sources and its manifold aspects, including the technical ones. It is not at all granted that technological innovations play a positive role, as they may well usher in the use of resources which are detrimental to the environment, with shale gas and tar sands being currently good examples.[5] Indeed, technological progress may become a big issue instead of a solution to the economic problems of a society of more than seven billion, as is widely automatically and implicitly assumed. Under this perspective there is no other possibility than for the government to redirect technological progress towards social welfare improvements. Since it is a private good it is driven by market forces, with no regard either for externalities or for the particular type of the natural resource involved. Another problem that must be addressed is that of the actual scarcity or relative abundance of the specific exhaustible resource considered. In other words, while oil and natural gas are predicted to be depleted in about 60–70 years if the present consumption rate continues (BP 2010: 6, 12), both coal and unconventional oil and gas are abundant and their depletion is not a concern. Thus while oil and natural gas prices are mainly driven by the scarcity rent this is not the case with the unconventional ones whose prices are mainly driven by production costs. The supply reaction to a demand-reducing climate policy, pointed out by Sinn, which gives rise to the GP, can be expected when the scarcity rent is so high that the resource price is well above costs (in fact Sinn 2012b considers it to be seven times as large as the unit extraction and exploration costs) and there is therefore enough margin to reduce the price and increase supply. When such margins do not exist the GP cannot emerge. It has actually been shown by Michielsen that in a world with imperfect substitution among 'one dirty and scarce fossil fuel (oil) and the other even dirtier and abundant (coal) ... the abundant dirty substitute reduces intertemporal leakage directly and indirectly and may even cause negative leakage rates' (Michielsen 2013: 2–3). In such a world a 'green orthodox', as he calls it, arises, in the sense that an anticipated environmental policy, namely a carbon tax, would reduce current emissions as the standard literature suggests. According to Michielsen the main reason for the theoretical emergence of a GP is that this literature does not take into due account the effects of (imperfect) climate policies on reducing the use of such dirty substitutes for oil and gas, like coal and unconventional oil, which are abundant and account for 50 per cent of current emissions. After the introduction of a carbon tax, coal and unconventional oil prices go up more than oil and gas prices, and the impact on future oil demand may well be to reduce it in favour of more demand for coal, which can be a better substitute for oil in the future as a consequence of technological improvements. This means that oil extraction will be delayed, not anticipated. In fact, since the 2008 seminal paper by Sinn a rich theoretical literature has thrived on the GP,[6] showing which ones are the most important elements to be considered when thinking of an effective climate policy, and shedding light on the complex mechanisms of reactions under different hypotheses which may or may not pre-empt the policy. All this turns out to be tremendously useful for the design of climate policy, which cannot do without the lessons from the theory of the GP, as well as from what the empirical evidence suggests about its practical occurrence.

Unfortunately, so far the empirical evidence literature is not as rich as the theoretical one, indeed it can count on just one paper by Di Maria et al. (2012). To test for the GP hypothesis the authors use the Acid Rain Program in the USA announced in 1990 and implemented in 1995. According to the GP theory, resource owners (coal in this case) would react to the announcement of the program by supplying more coal immediately and during the time between the announcement and the implementation of the program, which, by putting a nation-wide limit on sulphur dioxide emissions, was indeed a signal to the coal owners that after 1995 it would be difficult to sell their resources, and even more so for high-sulphur coal. The facts to be checked were therefore the following: (1) the decrease of the coal price that would have allowed the supply expansion, (2) the actual increase in coal use, and (3) the switching from low-sulphur to high-sulphur coal. Although the authors did find a reduction in the coal price, they also found that the sulphur content decreased (contradicting the hypothesis of a switching among different qualities of sulphur content coal, from cleaner to dirtier), and that few power plants responded to the price drop by using more coal. Indeed they conclude: 'on the face of this evidence, it seems that the answer to our title's question is a rather resounding "no"' (Di Maria et al. 2012: 1, 17). In other words although the mechanism depicted by the GP theory may be at work, 'market conditions and concurrent regulation prevented a GP from arising'.

While more empirical evidence is needed, it is clear that some market conditions are more important than others, and among these the price elasticity of demand is probably the main one. This is a natural conclusion since a drop in a depletable resource price does not automatically give way to a greater use of it, because the demand side plays a role too. While the GP hypothesis emerged mainly from observing that climate policies are meant to decrease the demand of fossil fuels without taking into account the possible supply reactions, the GP theory itself, which has the merit of considering the supply side, lacks adequate consideration of demand conditions such as price elasticity and imperfect substitutes.[7] If price elasticity of demand is very low the paradox does not arise, while if imperfect energy substitutes prevail both the weak and the strong paradox vanish (Gerlagh). The debate is open and the need for more empirical tests is unquestionable. Nevertheless some lessons are clear, and they must be heeded when trying to design efficient paradox-free climate policies.

Lessons from the Green Paradox literature

At present the literature on the GP is more on the side of not regarding it as a real threat of pre-empting climate policies, mainly because its occurrence is predicted within specific market and regulation conditions which are relatively unrealistic. Making more realistic hypotheses generally implies a weakening of the paradox and sometimes its vanishing. But the merit of this strand of recent literature is not just its warning that an imperfectly designed policy may backfire, but also its confirming once more the difficulties that the global community faces when dealing with climate change, which is a global externality. In order to cure it no country can stay outside a general agreement on the adoption of a policy that, needless to say, must be well designed and implemented in view of clearly specified targets. To this end some aspects are more important than others and some problems cannot be bypassed. Among them are the following.

First, the possible existence of a GP has contributed to a rethinking on policy design and target specification. Since the global warming effect (climate change) depends on the cumulative gas (CO_2) emitted, in order to stay within the limit indicated by the IPCC we cannot burn all the fossil fuel existing in the world, but must leave an amount unextracted.[8] Thus one has to think about what would be the best policy for leaving such an unextracted amount. In this respect a supply policy appears to be a good candidate for it can directly address the problem and therefore seems better suited for the target, instead of relying on the indirect effects of a demand policy. Moreover, we know from the GP literature that, at least in theory, a demand-reducing policy may cause the resource owners to anticipate extraction (intertemporal leakage), a fact that has to be avoided in order not to increase present emissions which increase the net present value of future damages (green welfare deterioration in the Gerlagh setting). On the contrary, what is needed is a policy capable of incentivizing extraction delay. Finally, avoiding anticipation in extraction is not all we need. Policy has somehow to steer the system towards choosing to leave the dirtiest resource unextracted, and this brings in the problem of technological evolution. It cannot be left completely to the market because we should use cheaper and cleaner substitute energy sources, while market-driven evolution of technology is not sensitive to society's need of using cleaner (and cheaper) energy sources. The type of technical progress that has made it possible to squeeze oil from tar sands and gas from shale is actually aggravating the problem of climate change instead of mitigating it.[9] The four predicaments here underlined – (1) leave a certain quantity unextracted, (2) avoid anticipated extraction by resource owners, (3) leave the dirtiest resources unextracted, (4) direct technological progress towards alleviation/mitigation of climate change – all seem to indicate a supply policy as the one that can directly attack the problems, much in line with Sinn's GP story.

Second, the time lapse between policy announcement and policy implementation is crucially important for the policy's effectiveness. It counts more than the design, in the sense that the longer the time between announcement of the introduction and actual introduction, the higher are the possibilities of adjusting supply and therefore of preempting any optimal or well-designed demand-reducing environmental policy. This aspect is of utmost importance, and it is not limited to demand policy, and not even to climate policy. Unfortunately, since it is tightly related to the decision-making process of contemporary democracies, complicated and lengthy even within a single country and more so when international negotiations are involved, it has general application. The longer the implementation lag, the greater the probabilities of reducing the impact of any government national and international intervention.

Third, although expectations about the policy stringency in the future may play a non-trivial role in the choice of the time path of extraction, the directions are not clear. According to the GP literature an expected stricter policy increases GP, but others hold different views. See for example Fischer and Salant (2012), Osterle (2012), Hoel (2011), and Van der Ploeg (2013). Moreover, it is not simply the expectation about the stringency of future policy that counts, but the pace at which it becomes stricter is even more important. This means that when for example the instrument adopted is a tax, its time path can cause the GP to occur or not to occur. Such opposite results are intuitive. Since this type of literature is based on the Hotelling model/logic, the rate of growth of the tax must be compared to the interest rate, and two cases are obviously possible: it may be greater or lower and hence give or not give rise to the GP (notice that the above arguments apply to the weak paradox only).

Fourth, the problem of the evolution of technical progress must be considered in combination with the policy chosen to reach the target. Even if the target of staying within the limit set by the IPCC is better served by a policy capable of inducing resource owners to leave a proper quantity of resource unburned, rather than by a policy aimed at curbing emissions by reducing fossil fuel demand (consumption), the problem of the types of resources to be left under the earth's crust remains unavoidable. A well-taken point by this strand of literature is that when assessing the policy impact on the basis of the Hotelling model, instead of assuming only one depletable source several different substitute sources must be considered. Substitutability conditions and different emissions potentials play important roles in terms of the policy impact. To mitigate climate change the dirtiest sources should be left under the earth's crust and for this result to be achieved the policy design should be precisely targeted to the purpose. Moreover, one cannot count on general technological evolution, because this responds to market conditions and fails to consider cleaner technologies. And even when market expectations about a more strict climate policy may play a positive role in steering technical progress towards the desirable direction, as was probably the case in the 'golden age' of environmental policy coinciding with the implementation of the Kyoto Protocol and the introduction of ETS in the EU, both events being signals of a growing international awareness of the need to combat global warming, it is still not enough. In fact the development of carbon capture and storage technology (CCS) may have been much encouraged by the Kyoto Protocol and the EU ETS, but its actual adoption is not granted. Thus we need to mandate it; otherwise resource owners will simply avoid the cost of adopting it. This means that the alternative to leave the necessary quantity unextracted, represented by the adoption of the CCS technology, does not come automatically from the market mechanism. And the same is true for the other possible alternative, represented by an increase in forest extension. In the case of forests, for instance, as we all know, market forces are pulling in the opposite direction. In the less developed countries, where they are more extended, forests are actually under threat of shrinking rather fast as they are subject to increasing cutting in response to the pressure of producing more crop both 'for table and for tank'. At the same time, rich countries, even those with an environmentally friendly past such as Canada, are now clearing their forests to collect tar sands and squeeze oil from them.[10] Current land use changes are definitely not helping with climate change.

Concluding remarks

Which policy do we need to pursue? It has to be *global* and with the smallest possible *time lapse* between announcement and implementation. Any departure from these two characteristics impairs results. In principle there are several alternatives. Four of them are listed here.

1. Introduce a global carbon tax (demand-side policy).
2. Introduce a global capital gains tax on energy resources (supply-side policy).
3. Mandate the adoption of CCS technology.
4. Stop deforestation and introduce afforestation plans.

All of them require cooperation among countries, to be translated into well-designed international treaties. The difficulties on the way to any kind of international agreements are well known. The suggestion would therefore be: choose the alternative with the greatest probability of being accepted by the global community. In this respect the second alternative, which in principle I would vote for as the best, looks like having the least probability of being accepted. Capital (gains) taxes are opposed by powerful lobbies and the not yet, if it ever will be, introduced global Tobin tax is an illuminating case. The fourth alternative has also a very low probability of being adopted, because it requires strong cooperation among rich and less developed countries, which proves to be a most difficult outcome given the huge differences among their economies. The CCS adoption would perhaps suffer from the same weakness of the fourth one, though to a lesser extent. Rich and less developed countries are in very different situations with respect to the adoption of new technologies, and this is not a good basis for building an international treaty. Finally, a global carbon tax still stands up as the best candidate,[11] especially if combined with a viable punishment for countries that do not participate in the treaty (or cheat it) in the form of a border tax adjustment (an import duty) on the carbon content of goods imported from countries with no carbon tax or no cap-and-trade system. The principal argument for opposing a carbon tax has always been the loss of competitiveness by the countries introducing a climate protection policy in the form of a carbon tax or an emissions trading system, which cause production costs to increase. Therefore in the global competition 'green countries', with a climate policy in place, would be disadvantaged in terms of production costs with respect to 'brown countries', with no climate policy or with a looser one. And this seems actually to be the case, as Sinn (2012a) clearly states. The spatial leakages predicted by the GP theory find their empirical confirmation in actual CO_2 emissions. As Figure 4.1 clearly depicts, CO_2 emissions by OECD countries show a non-increasing/decreasing trend which is more than compensated by the increasing trend in CO_2 emissions by the non-OECD countries (the overall trend is decisively increasing). By and large OECD countries are more sensitive to environmental protection than the non-OECD ones. Avoiding this effect is not impossible. A border tax adjustment of the type that does not violate World Trade Organization (WTO) agreements can do the job. Given the mission of the WTO, the watchdog of the free market, to control whether national governments provisions distort competitive conditions in the global market, a provision which aims at 'imposing the same or similar costs on *imports* as domestic climate policy imposes on *domestic* production' appears to be consistent and undisputable (Pauwelyn 2013: 449). In principle an import duty is considered feasible as far as it takes the form of an extension of internal carbon measures. Therefore a carbon tax or a cap-and-trade system in combination with border tax adjustments might be the practical solution to a much-needed global climate policy. No substantial obstacles appear to be left insofar as the competitiveness argument is overcome, but it all depends on whether countries are prepared to cooperate.

Can we expect countries to cooperate? The answer is no, both in theory (Finus 2002) and in practice. As soon as the number of subjects involved in a decision becomes large, cooperation fades away (see this book, Chapter 2) and the history of humankind shows no cooperation apart from small groups (families, tribes, and the like). Moreover in our globalized society conditions for cooperation are even weaker than in the past as the widespread trust in the free market has, first, obscured the role of the state, second, made the general public believe that there are alternatives to the state for the provision of public goods, and third, confused the notion itself of public goods, having popularized the two extreme and opposite views, equally wrong, of considering them either as actually 'commercial' or as 'common' goods in the sense of free access ones. Of course nothing can be free for society as a whole and not every good can be commercialized (clean air in cities, clean water in rivers, domestic safety in the ordinary life of ordinary people, national security, cannot). What the globalized society needs most is to rediscover the importance of the state. In the 1960s and 1970s economists were ready to provide counsel to policy-makers on the design of environmental policy on the basis of a clear and sound theory of externalities and public goods, and of what the market can do, or can do better than the government, and what it cannot. Fifty years on, we have moved backward behind where we were in the 1970s, and we need now to rediscover both the well-established *theory of externalities and public goods* and the *culture of the state*. Instead of moving forward society at large has moved backward, losing the civic culture of the state viewed as the only organization capable of bringing about the social welfare improving results that the intrinsic impossibility of large-scale voluntary cooperation prevents. Let us bring the culture of the state in from the cold (Chapter 1) and effectively face the environmental problems which threaten the very survival of human society.

Notes

1 Notice that the carbon leakage best known in the literature is in general produced by the strategic behaviour of the demand while here it is the strategic behaviour of resource owners that produces it. Notice also that here we have two types of carbon leakage: intertemporal and spatial.
2 It is also believed that pursuing a strategy of deep renovations of residential and commercial buildings towards energy efficiency may boost the development of new technological solutions and the creation of skilled jobs. In fact, the building stock is considered as the single biggest potential sector for energy saving and therefore the rate of building renovation needs to be increased (EU Directive 2012, amending EC Directives 2009/125/EC and EU Directive 2010/30/EU, and repealing directives EC Directive 2004/8/EC and 2006/32/EC).
3 This terminology, common among natural resource economists, is due to Nordhaus (1973).
4 Thus we face the same mechanism underlined by Sinn with reference to the tax. The introduction of a carbon tax induces the resource owner to anticipate extraction for fear of a decrease in its future returns. The use of subsidies to incentivize the introduction of cleaner energy produces the same reaction by the resource owner, namely the anticipation of extraction before the cleaner resource becomes cheaper and crowds out the dirtier one. In both cases the anticipation of extraction increases CO_2 emissions, which is the Green Paradox.
5 Unconventional oil is 20 per cent more emission-intensive than petroleum while coal is 30–40 per cent (Michielsen 2013).
6 A comprehensive survey of such literature is contained in Van der Werf and Di Maria (2012).

7 Actually introducing the demand side of the market may well lead to a weakening of the GP effects, which are emissions increases produced by well-intended but imperfectly implemented climate policies. According to Di Maria et al. (2013) this is the case: the demand side mitigates the increase in emissions.

8 According to Van der Ploeg (2013: 22) 'One trilllion tons of carbon must be either left unused or be sequestrated'.

9 Not surprisingly, the need to 'redirect technical change in the direction of green growth' is underlined by Van der Ploeg (2013).

10 Technical progress and forest extension are crucial ingredients for an effective climate policy (see this book, Chapters 7 and 8).

11 Or the equivalent global ETS.

References

Baumol, W. J. and Oates, W. E. 1988. *The Theory of Environmental Policy*, 2nd edn. Cambridge: Cambridge University Press (1st edn. 1975, Prentice-Hall).

BP. 2010. *Statistical Review of World Energy 2010*. London: BP.

Di Maria, C., Lange, I. and Van der Werf. E. 2012. 'Should We Be Worried about the Green Paradox? Announcement Effects of the Acid Rain Program'. CESifo Working Paper 3829.

Di Maria, C., Lange, I. and Van der Werf. E. 2013. 'Going Full Circle: Demand-Side Constraints to the Green Paradox'. CESifo Working Paper 4152.

European Commission. 1998. Directive on Fuel Quality 1998/70/EC.

European Commission. 2009. Directive on the Promotion of the Use of Energy from Renewable Resources 2009/28/EC.

European Union. 2012. Directive on Energy Efficiency 2012/2/EU.

Finus, M. 2002. 'Game Theory and International Environmental Cooperation: Any Practical Application?', in C. Bohringer, M. Finus, and C. Vogt (eds.), *Controlling Global Warming: Perspectives from Economics, Game Theory and Public Choice*. Cheltenham: Edward Elgar, pp. 9–104.

Fischer, C. and Salant, S. 2012. 'Alternative Climate Policies and Intertemporal Emissions Leakage: Quantifying the Green Paradox'. Resources for the Future Discussion Paper 12–16.

Gerlagh, R. 2011. 'Too Much Oil'. *CESifo Economic Studies*, 57: 79–102.

Herfindahl, O. C. 1967. 'Depletion and Economic Theory', in G. Mason (ed.), *Extractive Resources and Taxation*. Madison: University of Wisconsin Press, pp. 63–90.

Hoel, M. 2010. 'Is There a Green Paradox?' CESifo Working Paper 3168.

Hoel, M. 2011. 'The Green Paradox and Greenhouse Gas Reducing Investments'. *International Review of Environmental and Resource Economics*, 5(4): 353–79.

Hotelling, H. 1931. 'The Economics of Exhaustible Resources'. *Journal of Political Economy*, 39: 137–75.

IEA. 2012. *Emissions from Fuel Combustion 2012*. Paris: IEA.

Michielsen, T. 2013. 'Brown Backstop Versus the Green Paradox'. OxCarre Research Paper 108.

Nordhaus, W. 1973. 'The Allocation of Energy Reserves'. *Brookings Papers*, 3: 529–70.

Osterle, I. 2012. 'Fossil Fuel Extarction and Climate Policy: A Review of the Green Paradox with Endogenous Resource Exploration'. FEEM Nota di Lavoro 13.

Pauwelyn, J. 2013. 'Carbon Leakage Measures and Border Tax Adjustments under WTO Law', in D. Prevost and G. Van Calster (eds.), *Research Handbook on Environment, Health and the WTO*. Cheltenham: Edward Elgar, pp. 448–506.

Pearce, D. (ed.). 1989. *Blueprint for a Green Economy*. Abingdon: Earthscan.

Sinn, H.-W. 2008. 'Public Policies against Global Warming: A Supply Side Approach'. *International Tax and Public Finance*, 15: 360–94.

Sinn, H.-W. 2012a. *The Green Paradox: A Supply-Side Approach to Global Warming*. Cambridge, MA: MIT Press.

Sinn, H.-W. 2012b. 'The Green Paradox'. *The World Financial Review*, May–June.

Smulders, S., Tsur, Y., and Zemel, A. 2010. 'Announcing Climate Policy: Can a Green Paradox Arise without Scarcity?' CESifo Working Paper 3307.

United Nations. 1987. *Our Common Future* (The Brundtland Report). New York: United Nations.

Van der Ploeg, F. 2013. 'Cumulative Carbon Emissions and the Green Paradox'. OxCarre Research Paper 110.

Van der Ploeg, F. and Withagen, C. 2010. 'Is There Really a Green Paradox?' CESifo Working Paper 2963.

Van der Ploeg, F. and Withagen, C. 2013. 'Global Warming and the Green Paradox'. OxCarre Research Paper 116.

Van der Werf, E. and Di Maria, C. 2012. 'Imperfect Environmental Policy and Polluting Emissions: The Green Paradox and Beyond'. *International Review of Environmental and Resource Economics*, 6: 153–94.

5 Environmental policy-making in real life

Illegal waste disposal in the presence of organized crime

Alessio D'Amato and Mariangela Zoli

Introduction

This chapter deals with the role of the public sector in coping with environmental issues, with a specific focus on waste management. The waste sector is a field of particular interest to analyze government intervention in the economy. Of course, we do not aim at analyzing all possible arguments justifying public intervention in this sector. We focus instead on a particular aspect of the waste management system, related to the emergence of possible illegal behaviors and the presence of organized crime. By developing a theoretical model where illegal waste disposal and criminal organizations are explicitly admitted, we analyze the implications of different environmental tax designs in terms of waste management decisions and Mafia entry incentives.

The starting point of our analysis is the Polluter-Pays Principle, a fundamental principle of environmental policy for both the OECD and the European Community which underpins most pollution regulations affecting land, water, and air. According to this principle, the costs of pollution should be borne by those who produce it. Several examples of its application in European environmental legislation can be found. The Water Framework Directive (2000/60/EC), for instance, calls for "the recovery of the costs of water services, including environmental and resource costs associated with damage or negative impact on the aquatic environment, in accordance with the polluter-pays principle," specifying, in particular, that all water users (industry, households, and agriculture) must make "adequate contributions" to the recovery of such costs (art. 9). The full cost recovery is required also by the Landfill Directive (99/31/EC), where it is specified that "all of the costs involved in the setting up and operation of a landfill site ... and the estimated costs of the closure and after-care of the site for a period of at least 30 years shall be covered by the price to be charged by the operator for the disposal of any type of waste in that site" (art. 10). In this spirit, the Italian Environmental Code (Codice dell'ambiente, Dlgs 152/2006) requires that waste management operations satisfy a budget balancing condition. All previous examples show that while the Polluter-Pays Principle recalls the Pigouvian theory according to which polluters must pay a unit tax equal to the marginal environmental damage, its application in actual environmental policy seems to differ, being interpreted more as a cost recovery condition.

The adoption of the cost recovery principle rather than a Pigouvian tax has different effects on waste disposal decisions in a context where organized crime can enter the waste cycle. In the theoretical model we present in this chapter, we first investigate the impact of the adoption of the two tax regimes in terms of legal disposal and illegal dumping choices by the regulated agent. Then we focus on the role of organized crime, in order to assess which tax regime provides stronger incentives to the Mafia's entry in waste management. We also achieve counterintuitive results concerning the impact of organized crime on social welfare.

The rest of the chapter is structured as follows. The next section provides an introductory framework which describes the main issues related to waste management problems and the limits to collective action and public regulation in this sector. Afterwards, we introduce the theoretical model and we compare different waste policy regimes. Some concluding remarks are provided in the final section.

Conceptual framework

Current waste production levels and methods of disposal are a typical example of the negative externalities stemming from production and consumption activities. Despite increasing awareness of the social and environmental costs of waste generation, municipal solid waste has grown dramatically over the last decades as a result of higher incomes, more intensive use of packaging materials, and increased purchases of durable material goods (Ferrara and Missios 2012). As highlighted in a recent work by the World Bank, global levels of municipal solid waste (MSW) generation are expected to increase from the current 1.3 billion tonnes per year to approximately 2.2 billion tonnes per year by 2025, corresponding to an increase in per capita waste generation from 1.2 to 1.42 kg per person per day (Hoornweg and Bhada-Tata 2012). This increasing trend characterizes both developed and developing countries. Within the OECD region, MSW production increased by about 58 per cent from 1980 to 2000 (corresponding to an average growth rate of 2.5 per cent) and by 4.6 per cent between 2000 and 2005 (+0.9 per cent per year). On the basis of these trends and in the absence of new correct-ive policies, total municipal waste is projected to increase by 38 per cent from 2005 to 2030 (OECD 2008a). Estimated waste quantities are expected to increase considerably also in developing countries, and in 2030 the non-OECD area is expected to produce about 70 per cent of the world's municipal waste, as a consequence of the rapid rate of urban-ization and technical and economic development[1] (OECD 2008b).

Waste collection and disposal harm the environment and impose external costs on society (in addition to private costs for individuals as well as local authorities that typically manage municipal solid waste disposal operations). The extent of the threat posed to the environment depends also on the method of waste management that is adopted. As highlighted in the so-called "waste hierarchy,"[2] which classifies waste management strategies on the basis of their environmental impact, reduction and re-use are the most preferred options,[3] allowing for the saving of natural resources and pollution reduction, followed by recyc-ling and composting, energy recovery, and, lastly, treatment and dis-posal, which are considered as the last resort and should be reduced. The external costs of landfills are now widely known: besides problems with odor, noise, and litter, which affect primarily nearby residents, landfills can be hazardous to health and to the environment, due to emissions of methane and carbon dioxide (which contribute to local pollution, as well as to global pollution and global warming[4]), and leakages of dan-gerous substances such as metals and chemicals into the groundwater.[5] Indeed, landfilling is still the most common method of MSW disposal worldwide,[6] while recycling and even more reduction have led only to minor achievements. By limiting our attention to European member states, it can be noted that while significant improvements in recycling performance have been realized since the adoption of the EU strat-egy on the prevention and recycling of waste in 2005, the amounts of municipal waste generated are still not decreasing (Eurostat 2013; EEA 2013). This suggests that the set of economic incentives introduced by legislation (tax and charges, as well as extended producer responsibility policies) have proved partly effective in encouraging recycling but quite ineffective in promoting waste prevention (Cecere et al. 2013).

Several theoretical and empirical papers have investigated how waste management decisions can be affected by government policies (for a review of the theoretical economic literature on this issue see, for instance, Choe and Fraser 1998; Fullerton and Kinnaman 2002; Ferrara 2008). In order to be effective, however, policy instruments should take into account that the environmental quality that would result from optimal choices of waste production and disposal has public good characteristics,[7] exhibiting both non-excludability and consumption indivisibilities (Tietenberg and Lewis 2012). In other words, nobody can be excluded from enjoying the benefits of proper waste management once it has been put in place (even those who fail to "pay" for it), and consumption of these benefits by one person does not reduce the amount available for others. In this context, and by considering that waste reduction and recycling behaviors are costly for individuals, it can be expected that the environmental quality coming from a proper waste management system would be undersupplied, since individuals who bear the costs do not enjoy all the benefits of their actions. Consider, for instance, the environmental benefits produced by a reduction in the amount of waste sent to landfills: households bearing the (private) costs of proper disposal and recycling decisions are not necessarily those that enjoy such benefits directly[8] (if they do not live nearby a landfill, for example) or (even if they live near the landfill) they do not have the exclusive right to enjoy these benefits.

This divergence between individuals who benefit and individuals who pay the cost of the environmental quality, as well as the plurality of agents involved in the waste cycle, contributes to explaining the misallocation of waste and calls for corrective public intervention.

As argued above, in recent years governments have introduced legislation intended to divert waste from landfills and increase recycling, as well as policy initiatives, such as the introduction of landfill taxes and unit charges for garbage collection services, in order to correct waste misallocation.

The investigation of the efficiency and effectiveness properties of public intervention in the waste sector, however, is further complicated once the possibility of illegal disposal is explicitly admitted.

Though some illegal disposal may happen even without any waste pricing scheme, when charges on legal disposal are introduced, illegal disposal becomes undoubtedly a major social problem (Porter 2002). This is shown by several examples in different countries: the Scotland Environmental Protection Agency (SEPA), for instance, has explicitly recognized that the increase of landfill taxes has resulted in the growth of illegal landfills across Scotland, a lucrative affair leading to multi-million pound landfill tax-evasion.[9] A positive relationship between the strictness of waste policy and illegal disposal is also proved to exist in Italy by D'Amato et al. (2014), where it is shown that a stronger municipality commitment towards waste management tends to favor the emergence of illegal disposal.

Optimal policy instruments, then, will be different when there is the possibility of illegal waste disposal or when we admit, more realistically, that organized crime can directly manage the waste treatment by distorting the waste cycle. There is increasing international evidence showing that waste mismanagement is the result of complex interactions at different levels among politicians and bureaucrats, organized crime and entrepreneurs, each of them receiving a reward from illegal waste management. As argued by Liddick (2010), by the late twentieth century, as tighter waste regulation increased the costs of legal disposal, organized transnational criminals, corporate polluters, and corrupt public officials engaged in an illicit traffic whose scope and profitability are now rivalling the international drugs trade. In several cases, illegal waste disposal is enabled by conniving local authorities, and also corrupt practices at high levels of government. Liddick (2011), for instance, reports the case of 15,000 tons of toxic incinerator ash produced in Philadelphia and dumped in Guinea by a Norwegian firm, having been (mis)labeled as material for brick-making. The Norwegian Consul General and other government officials were implicated in this deal (Liddick 2011).

In the case of Italy, there is a large body of evidence testifying to the role of criminal organizations in the waste management cycle. As witnessed by anecdotal evidence related to the waste crisis in the southern Italian regions (see, among others, D'Alisa et al. 2010; Pasotti 2010), interactions among waste producers, corrupt local authorities, supervisory bodies, and the local Mafia give rise to sophisticated illegal systems for falsifying transport and processing documents, which undermine the correct management of waste collection and disposal (Legambiente 2010, 2011, 2012; Massari and Monzini 2004).

Despite this evidence, however, only very recently has the economic literature started to investigate (both theoretically and empirically) the role of organized crime in waste management. D'Amato and Zoli (2012), for instance, explicitly model a criminal organization which extorts (socially costly) rent from agents willing to perform illegal disposal. Their main findings suggest that, under certain conditions, the Mafia presence can lead to increased levels of economic activity and lower levels of enforcement; in some cases, the related benefits may offset the damages from increased illegal disposal and the social costs of Mafia rents. The relevance of illegal disposal and criminal organizations is also suggested by D'Amato et al. (2011), where empirical results show that legal disposal and recyclable waste levels are affected negatively by the presence of Mafia type organizations.

Differently from previous contributions, the model presented in the following section provides a theoretical framework to explore the consequences of different tax designs in terms of legal/illegal waste disposal decisions and entry incentives for Mafia type organizations.

The theoretical model

An economic agent (a consumer or a firm) performs an (exogenously given) economic activity, y; such activity generates waste that can be disposed of legally (the corresponding amount being g) or illegally (b). Legal disposal implies some private costs for the firm in terms of bureaucratic steps (form-filling, authorizations, waste storage, transport, etc.). This first category of costs implicitly allows for the existence of other actors (e.g. transport and treatment firms for toxic waste) which are not explicitly modeled in our setting. A second kind of cost for legal disposal is borne by local public entities that take care of waste management and disposal (for example municipal solid waste collection, landfilling related costs, etc.). Finally, a third category of costs are related to externalities stemming from legal disposal (e.g. in terms of emissions from landfilling and incineration). In our setting, overall costs of legal waste disposal (including all the three above categories) are given by an increasing and convex function $\varepsilon(g)$. To disentangle the different relevant cost types, we assume that firm's private costs of legal disposal (i.e. the above-mentioned first category) are an (exogenous) fraction α of overall costs. The fraction $(1-\alpha)$ represents therefore social costs, related both to management and disposal activities as well as to environmental damages.

The firm also pays a unit tax t (for example a landfill tax) on legal disposal, while illegal disposal implies an expected payment (p) which depends on the presence or absence of a criminal organization in the waste cycle, as shown below. As waste must be disposed of in some way, we can conclude that $b = y - g$, and the agent's cost minimization problem can be written as follows:

$$\min_{g} \alpha\varepsilon(g) + tg + p(y - g) \tag{1}$$

As a result, first-order conditions are:[10]

$$\alpha\varepsilon_g(.) + t - p = 0.$$

Straightforward comparative statics implies $\dfrac{dg}{dt} < 0$ and $\dfrac{dg}{dp} = -\dfrac{dg}{dt} > 0$. In what follows, we assume that ε_{gg} is constant to rule out the possibility that results depend on higher-order derivatives.

Comparing environmental tax regimes

Optimal taxation

This is our benchmark case. When organized crime is not present, the expected payment for illegal disposal is given by an expected fine V (so that $p = V$). The fine sums up exogenous monitoring and enforcement effort exerted by a public police authority.[11] In the "optimal tax" scenario, the waste tax is set to minimize total waste-related social costs, which are given by:

$$W = \varepsilon(g) + \delta(b) \tag{2}$$

where $\delta(.)$ is an increasing and convex function representing the social costs of illegal disposal, related for instance to health damage due to improper discharge of dangerous substances.[12] The first-order conditions for the optimal tax rate require:[13]

$$\delta_b(y \text{-} g^*) = \varepsilon_g(g^*), \tag{3}$$

which identifies the first best level of legal (and illegal) disposal.[14]

Comparative statics is easily shown to imply $\dfrac{dt^*}{dV} = 1$, that is, enforcement and the optimal tax rate are perfect complements: a unit increase in enforcement implies the same increase in the tax rate to keep legal disposal constant at its first best level.

Coherently with Garoupa (2000), when the Mafia is present, we assume that enforcement is devoted to the waste producer, while the Mafia cannot be punished.

The expected payment for the regulated agent is, in this case, $p = V + x$, where x is the extortion fee required by the Mafia on each unit of illegal disposal.[15]

The Mafia is assumed to be a rent maximizing entity, bearing fixed costs K to infiltrate the local institutions. As a result, the rent maximization problem can be written as:

$$\max_x R = xb - K \tag{4}$$

First-order conditions are as follows:[16]

$$b + b_x(.)x = 0.$$

Under our assumption of constant ε_{gg}, comparative statics implies: $\dfrac{dx}{dt} = \dfrac{1}{2}$, and $\dfrac{dx}{dV} = -\dfrac{1}{2}$.

Minimization of (2) requires, again, (3) to hold.[17] As a result, optimal legal and illegal disposal amounts are the same as in the absence of the Mafia and $dt = dV$, as in the no Mafia case.

Full cost recovery

We now turn to the case where the environmental tax is set to cover the social costs related to legal disposal, including both management and external costs.[18] Under our assumptions, we must have $tg = (1-\alpha)\varepsilon(g)$, or:

$$t^F = (1-\alpha)\frac{\varepsilon(g^F)}{g^F} \tag{5}$$

(the superscript F denotes the full cost recovery equilibrium values). This condition applies both in the absence and in the presence of the Mafia, although we can expect it to lead to different tax and legal disposal levels in the two scenarios. To achieve readable insights, we now put more structure in the model and revert to specific functional forms.

A tractable example

To investigate social welfare impacts and to address the incentives of the Mafia to enter the waste cycle, let us assume:

$$\varepsilon(g) = \alpha\varepsilon\frac{g^2}{2} + (1-\alpha)\varepsilon\frac{g^2}{2} = \varepsilon\frac{g^2}{2}, \quad \delta(y-g) = \delta\frac{(y-g)^2}{2}, \quad \text{where} \quad \varepsilon > 0$$

and $\delta > 0$

The agent's cost minimization problem can therefore be rewritten as follows:

$$\min_{g} \alpha\varepsilon\frac{g^2}{2} + tg + p(y-g).$$

As a result, the legal disposal level is:

$$g = \frac{1}{\alpha\varepsilon}(p-t)$$

where $p = V$ in the absence of the Mafia, while $p = x + V$ with the Mafia.

In the absence of the Mafia, the optimal tax minimizes overall social costs which, in our quadratic specification, are given by:

$$SC = \varepsilon \frac{g^2}{2} + \delta \frac{(y - g)^2}{2} \tag{6}$$

First-order necessary and sufficient conditions require:

$$t_n^* = V - \frac{y \alpha \delta \varepsilon}{\delta + \varepsilon},$$

(we label the no Mafia cases with subscript n). The above tax rate leads to the following equilibrium level of legal disposal:

$$g_n^* = y \frac{\delta}{\delta + \varepsilon}.$$

Turning to the full cost recovery tax scenario, condition (5) requires, limiting our attention to strictly positive values for g and t:

$$t_n^F = V \frac{(1 - \alpha)}{1 + \alpha}.$$

The resulting level of legal disposal is:

$$g_n^F = 2 \frac{V}{\varepsilon (\alpha + 1)}.$$

When the Mafia is present (i.e. $p = V + x$), it maximizes the net rent from illegal disposal, given by the extortion rate (x) *times* the level of illegal disposal:[19]

$$R = \max_x x(y - g) \tag{7}$$

The corresponding necessary and sufficient condition is given by:

$$\left(-\frac{2}{\alpha \varepsilon} \right) x + \left(y - \frac{1}{\alpha \varepsilon} (V - t) \right) = 0,$$

so that the extortion rate, for any given V, is:

$$x = \frac{1}{2}(t - V + y\alpha\varepsilon).$$

As a result, the payment for illegal disposal for any given V and t is as follows:

$$p = \frac{1}{2}(t + V + y\alpha\varepsilon)$$

which is now a function of t. This is expected to generate a distortion in legal waste taxation as compared to the no Mafia case. In other words, the tax design can affect welfare and Mafia entry incentives.

Under an optimal taxation regime, the regulator chooses again the tax rate to minimize social costs, given in (6). The corresponding necessary and sufficient conditions for a minimum lead to the following tax rate:

$$t_m^* = V - y\alpha\varepsilon \frac{(\delta - \varepsilon)}{\delta + \varepsilon},$$

implying the following levels of legal disposal and extortion rate, respectively:

$$g_m^* = y\frac{\delta}{\delta + \varepsilon},$$

coherently with results in the "optimal taxation" section above, and

$$x^* = y\alpha \frac{\varepsilon^2}{\delta + \varepsilon}.$$

Under a full cost recovery tax rate, condition (5) implies (again excluding the tax rate level that drives g to 0),

$$t_m^F = \frac{1 - \alpha}{3\alpha + 1}(V + y\alpha\varepsilon),$$

and the corresponding levels of legal disposal and extortion rate are, respectively:

$$g_m^F = \frac{2(V + y\alpha\varepsilon)}{\varepsilon(3\alpha + 1)}$$

and

$$x^F = \frac{\alpha}{3\alpha+1}\left(y\varepsilon(1+\alpha)-2V\right).$$

Table 5.1 sums up equilibrium values under the four modeled scenarios.

Positive values for equilibrium variables under all scenarios require $V > \frac{y\alpha\delta\varepsilon}{\delta+\varepsilon}$ (which guarantees positive optimal tax rates both in the absence and in the presence of the Mafia) and $V < \frac{1}{2}y\varepsilon(\alpha+1)$ (in order for the extortion rate and illegal disposal levels arising under the two full cost recovery scenarios to be positive). These two inequalities can indeed hold at the same time, as $\frac{1}{2}y\varepsilon(\alpha+1)-\frac{y\alpha\delta\varepsilon}{\delta+\varepsilon} = \frac{1}{2}y\varepsilon\left(1-\alpha\frac{\delta-\varepsilon}{\delta+\varepsilon}\right)$, while $\delta-\varepsilon < \delta+\varepsilon$ and $\alpha < 1$, so that $\alpha\frac{\delta-\varepsilon}{\delta+\varepsilon} < 1$ and $\left(1-\alpha\frac{\delta-\varepsilon}{\delta+\varepsilon}\right) > 0$; therefore, we simply have to assume $\frac{y\alpha\delta\varepsilon}{\delta+\varepsilon} < V < \frac{1}{2}y\varepsilon(\alpha+1)$.

By inspecting Table 5.1, we can notice that, coherently with the previous sections' results, both the optimal and the full cost recovery tax rates are larger with the Mafia than in its absence; this is straightforward concerning optimal taxation, while under full cost recovery it is easily shown that $t_m^F - t_n^F = \alpha(1-\alpha)\frac{y\varepsilon(1+\alpha)-2V}{(\alpha+1)(3\alpha+1)} > 0$, where the inequality stems from the assumption that $V < \frac{1}{2}y\varepsilon(\alpha+1)$. Also, the level of legal and illegal disposal is the same, independently of the presence of the Mafia, under optimal taxation; this is the result of a larger payment for illegal disposal under the Mafia, which under optimal taxation is perfectly offset by an increase in the tax rate. Under full cost recovery, legal disposal is larger (i.e. illegal disposal is smaller) with the Mafia, as $g_m^F - g_n^F = 2\alpha\frac{y\varepsilon(1+\alpha)-2V}{\varepsilon(\alpha+1)(3\alpha+1)} > 0$. In the latter case, the increase in the payment for illegal disposal under the Mafia more than counterbalances the larger tax rate arising under full cost recovery when the Mafia is present. This is a first important point stemming from our

Table 5.1 Equilibrium values

	Waste tax	Legal disposal	Extortion
Optimal – no Mafia	$V - \dfrac{y\alpha\delta\varepsilon}{\delta+\varepsilon}$	$y\dfrac{\delta}{\delta+\varepsilon}$	–
Optimal – Mafia	$V - y\alpha\varepsilon\dfrac{(\delta-\varepsilon)}{\delta+\varepsilon}$	$y\dfrac{\delta}{\delta+\varepsilon}$	$y\alpha\dfrac{\varepsilon^2}{\delta+\varepsilon}$
Full cost – no Mafia	$V\dfrac{(1-\alpha)}{1+\alpha}$	$2\dfrac{V}{\varepsilon(\alpha+1)}$	–
Full cost – Mafia	$\dfrac{1-\alpha}{3\alpha+1}(V+y\alpha\varepsilon)$	$\dfrac{2(V+y\alpha\varepsilon)}{\varepsilon(3\alpha+1)}$	$\dfrac{\alpha(y\varepsilon(1+\alpha)-2V)}{3\alpha+1}$

Note: "Optimal" stands for optimal taxation and "Full Cost" stands for full cost recovery.

analysis: the choice of the objective (full cost recovery vs. Pigouvian taxation) hugely affects the impact of taxation in terms of legal and illegal disposal. Surprisingly, "total" enforcement is stronger in the presence of the Mafia.[20] Turning to the incentives for organized crime to enter the waste cycle, we define the Mafia's rent as:

$$R_m^* = x^* \left(y - g_m^* \right) = y^2\alpha \frac{\varepsilon^3}{\left(\delta+\varepsilon\right)^2}$$

under the optimal tax, and

$$R_m^F = x^F \left(y - g_m^F \right) = \alpha \frac{\left(2V - y\varepsilon(1+\alpha)\right)^2}{\varepsilon(3\alpha+1)^2}$$

under full cost recovery. By comparing equilibrium variables and Mafia rents under optimal taxation and full cost recovery, we get the following proposition:

Proposition 1. In the presence of the Mafia, under relatively large damages from illegal disposal and a sufficiently weak enforcement, full cost recovery taxation implies (as compared to optimal taxation) a larger illegal disposal, extortion, and tax rate as well as a larger Mafia rent.

Proof. Comparing equilibrium values under the two taxation regimes in the presence of organized crime, as well as the net rent accruing to the Mafia, we get:

$$g_m^* - g_m^F = -\frac{\left(2V(\delta+\varepsilon) - y\delta\varepsilon(\alpha+1) + 2y\alpha\varepsilon^2\right)}{\varepsilon(\delta+\varepsilon)(3\alpha+1)};$$

$$t_m^* - t_m^F = 2\alpha\frac{\left(2V(\delta+\varepsilon) - y\delta\varepsilon(\alpha+1) + 2y\alpha\varepsilon^2\right)}{(3\alpha+1)(\delta+\varepsilon)};$$

$$x^* - x^F = \alpha\frac{\left(2V(\delta+\varepsilon) - y\delta\varepsilon(\alpha+1) + 2y\alpha\varepsilon^2\right)}{(3\alpha+1)(\delta+\varepsilon)};$$

and

$$R_m^* - R_m^F = -\alpha\left(2V(\delta+\varepsilon) - y\delta\varepsilon(\alpha+1) + 2y\alpha\varepsilon^2\right)$$
$$\times \frac{2V(\delta+\varepsilon) - y\varepsilon(\delta+2\varepsilon+\alpha\delta+4\alpha\varepsilon)}{\varepsilon(\delta+\varepsilon)^2(3\alpha+1)^2}.$$

Notice that $2V(\delta+\varepsilon) - y\delta\varepsilon(\alpha+1) + 2y\alpha\varepsilon^2 > 0$ requires $V > V_m = \dfrac{y\varepsilon}{2(\delta+\varepsilon)}(\delta(1+\alpha) - 2\alpha\varepsilon)$, while $2V(\delta+\varepsilon) - y\varepsilon(\delta+2\varepsilon+\alpha\delta+4\alpha\varepsilon) > 0$ if $V > V_r = y\dfrac{\varepsilon}{2(\delta+\varepsilon)}(\delta+2\varepsilon+\alpha\delta+4\alpha\varepsilon)$.

Also, it is easily shown that $V_r - \dfrac{1}{2}y\varepsilon(\alpha+1) > 0$, so that our assumption that $V < \dfrac{1}{2}y\varepsilon(\alpha+1)$ implies that it is always $V < V_r$. Further, while $V_m < \dfrac{1}{2}y\varepsilon(\alpha+1)$, so that $V > V_m$ is always feasible, in order for $V < V_m$ to be possible, we must have $V_m > \dfrac{y\alpha\delta\varepsilon}{\delta+\varepsilon}$, that is $\dfrac{\delta}{\varepsilon} > \dfrac{2\alpha}{1-\alpha} > 0$. Finally, $V_m < V_r$. As a result, if $\dfrac{\delta}{\varepsilon} > \dfrac{2\alpha}{1-\alpha}$ we can have two cases:

1. if $V < V_m$, then $g_m^* > g_m^F, t_m^* < t_m^F, x^* < x^F$ and $R_m^* < R_m^F$
2. if $V > V_m$, then $g_m^* < g_m^F, t_m^* > t_m^F, x^* > x^F$ and $R_m^* > R_m^F$.

On the other hand, if $\dfrac{\delta}{\varepsilon} < \dfrac{2\alpha}{1-\alpha}$, then we are left with case 2, as it is always $V > V_m$.

Under Mafia and full cost recovery, as V decreases, the extortion fee increases but not enough to compensate the reduction in V, so that the total payment for illegal disposal decreases. Such reduction is larger (in absolute terms) than the corresponding reduction in the waste tax. As a result, illegal disposal increases. The overall outcome is a stronger entry incentive for the Mafia. Under optimal taxation, an increase in V always implies an identical increase in t. Illegal disposal, extortion, and the Mafia rent are therefore not affected. Thus, a sufficiently low V exists such that the rent under full cost recovery is larger than the one arising under optimal taxation. However, the latter case vanishes when damages from illegal disposal are relatively low and then the optimal tax rate can be set without worrying too much about illegal disposal.

Interesting results also arise comparing social costs under full cost recovery, in the absence and in the presence of the Mafia, given that the first best is by definition the minimum social costs allocation. Indeed, evaluating social costs from (6) in the full cost recovery equilibria, respectively in the absence of the Mafia (labeled as SC_m^F) and in its presence (labeled as SC_n^F), we can conclude that $SC_m^F < SC_n^F$ for

$$V < V_s = \frac{1}{2} y \varepsilon \frac{(\alpha + 1)(\delta + \alpha(2\delta - \varepsilon))}{(\delta + \varepsilon)(2\alpha + 1)}.$$ Of course, for this to be possible

we must assume $V_s > \dfrac{y\alpha\delta\varepsilon}{\delta + \varepsilon}$, that is: $\dfrac{\delta}{\varepsilon} > \dfrac{\alpha(\alpha + 1)}{(1 - \alpha)(2\alpha + 1)}$.[21]

We get therefore the following proposition:

Proposition 2. The full cost recovery equilibrium can be closer to first best in the presence of the Mafia than in its absence. This is the case when enforcement is sufficiently weak and social costs from illegal disposal (legal disposal) are sufficiently large (small).

The driving forces of the last result are mainly related to marginal social costs arising from legal and illegal disposal. Figure 5.1 (top) shows the case when enforcement is relatively weak:[22] full cost recovery in the presence of the Mafia implies that legal disposal is closer to first best than when the Mafia is not present. As a result, when a full cost recovery tax is adopted, the presence of the Mafia implies lower social costs.

Figure 5.1 (bottom) shows a case of relatively strong enforcement.[23] In such a case, the Mafia may be disruptive under full cost recovery even if it generates a smaller illegal disposal (i.e. a larger legal disposal), due for example to the possible presence of significant capacity constraints on the legal disposal side (e.g. due to scarcity of land).

Proposition 2 is interesting as it suggests that, if a full cost recovery scheme is adopted, then the presence of the Mafia can improve social costs when enforcement is sufficiently weak. Furthermore, and contrary to the existing literature (Garoupa 2000, among others), we show that the impact of organized crime on social welfare does not necessarily depend on ad hoc hypotheses (like introducing social disruption related to violence, etc.); welfare impacts may indeed depend only on the presence of convexities in damage costs, which is a quite reasonable assumption in dealing with environmental issues.

Concluding remarks

In this chapter we have addressed the issue of government intervention to correct environmental problems with specific reference to the waste sector. Our background arguments rely on the public goods characteristics of the environmental quality resulting from proper waste management and disposal decisions. Non-excludability from the benefits of correct waste behaviors and the emergence of free-rider incentives, arising from the fact that individuals may enjoy the benefits of a good environmental quality without contributing to its costs, may lead to "undersupply" of recycling and waste reduction activities. In this context, public intervention is required to stimulate households' and firms' behaviors towards more sustainable waste management decisions. Under this perspective, government intervention should be designed in order to provide, on the one side, proper monetary and non-monetary incentives to individuals to affect their waste decisions and, on the other side, to structure the waste management system coherently with the waste hierarchy, by reducing the amount sent to landfill and incineration and promoting reduction, re-use, and recycling. Addressing this issue is particularly challenging if we consider that waste generation has grown significantly over the last decades and does not seem to reverse this trend (as the data provided in this chapter suggest), but at the same time particularly pressing. Even though awareness of the external effects of waste production and disposal is increasing, current models of goods production and consumption have not yet been modified to fully account for their environmental consequences.

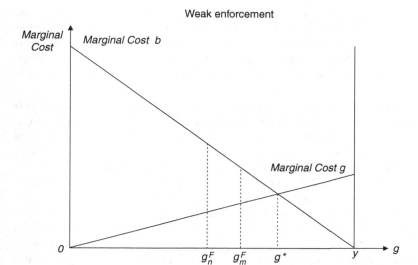

Weak enforcement

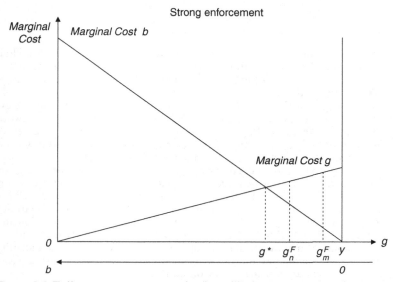

Strong enforcement

Figure 5.1 Full cost recovery vs. optimal equilibria. Top: Weak enforcement; Bottom: Strong enforcement

Another specificity we addressed refers to the features of the waste sector that make this sector particularly at risk of corruption and criminal activity. When illegal disposal is present and criminal organizations may enter the waste cycle, opportunities for public interventions to correct individual behaviors and design sound waste policies are seriously reduced.

Starting from these considerations, our theoretical model in this chapter aimed explicitly at modeling the effects of two different environmental policy designs in a context characterized by illegal disposal and organized crime. Specifically, we have shown that, in a realistic framework where public authorities exert also (exogenous) enforcement efforts to contrast illegal dumping, the choice of the policy regime (namely, either full cost recovery or optimal taxation) is not neutral in terms of incentives for illegal disposal and for Mafia entry. Such conclusions can be interpreted as additional theoretical support to the idea that criminal waste behavior can significantly affect waste and, more generally, environmental policy design. Public intervention in the environmental realm has to find ways to deal with these additional hurdles. In this work we hope to have provided some food for thought in this direction.

Notes

1 In 2030, for instance, China is expected to generate at least 485 million tonnes (up 214 per cent from 2004) of MSW, while in India the corresponding amount will be around 250 million tonnes (up 130 per cent from 2001) (OECD 2008b).
2 The "waste hierarchy" is at the core of waste policies in several countries. At the EU level, for instance, it has been introduced by the Waste Framework Directive in 2008 (art. 4). To move up the waste hierarchy, member states are required to establish national waste prevention programs and to set out appropriate specific targets to assess their progress (art. 29).
3 In response to the challenges posed by growing waste volumes, the concept of reduction/prevention of waste generation has been developed in major international conventions and public policies on waste management. The Basel Convention on the Control of Transboundary Movements of Hazardous Wastes and their Disposal, the Organisation for Economic Co-operation and Development (OECD), the European Environment Agency (EEA), and the United States Environmental Protection Agency (EPA), for instance, identify minimization as one of the key instruments to counter the growing waste problem (Secretariat of the Basel Convention 2012).
4 Global greenhouse gas (GHG) emissions from MSW are estimated to account for almost 5 per cent (1,460 mtCO$_2$e) of total GHG emissions (Hoornweg and Bhada-Tata 2012).
5 Among the various estimates of the externalities coming from landfill and incineration see, for instance, European Commission (2000); Turner et al. (2004); Powell and Brisson (1994); Ham et al. (2013).

6 See, for instance, figure 11 (p. 22) in Hoornweg and Bhada-Tata (2012).
7 As Pearce (2004: 115) notes, "many environmental problems have regional or even global public good (or public bad) characteristics."
8 Direct benefits resulting from landfill reduction entail reduced health impacts, lower losses of property values, avoided ecosystem losses, and other welfare effects that have mainly a local dimension, benefiting mainly individuals living nearby the landfills. Benefits, such as prevention of pollution and climate change effects that have a global dimension, tend to be underestimated by individuals when they take waste management decisions.
9 Interview of the Scotland Environmental Protection Agency (SEPA) chairman David Sigsworth to *The Herald* newspaper. See http://www.herald-scotland.com/news/crime-courts/dirty-money.21465337, accessed October 20, 2013.
10 Notice that we rule out the uninteresting case where $b = 0$. Also, notice that private illegal disposal costs are normalized to 0.
11 In this simplified setting, we keep enforcement exogenous to focus on the role played by waste-related taxation.
12 Notice that, as in Fullerton and Kinnaman (1995), our first best setting implies that illegal disposal cannot be taxed directly by the regulator.
13 Convexity requires: $\varepsilon_{gg}(g^*) + \delta_{bb}(y - g^*) > 0$ which always holds.
14 First best can be obtained in the presence of illegal disposal as a direct consequence of assuming exogenous enforcement.
15 The assumption that the Mafia cannot be punished (i.e. the expected fine is paid by the agent, $p = V + x$) does not affect the results, except for the impact of changes of V on x. As we show below, under $p = V + x$ the extortion fee decreases with V (i.e. $\frac{dx}{dV} = -\frac{1}{2}$). At the opposite, assuming that the Mafia hides illegal behavior by the agent, i.e. $p = x$, would only imply that the equilibrium extortion fee increases with enforcement, i.e. $\frac{dx}{dV} = \frac{1}{2}$. However, it is easily shown that $\frac{dp}{dV} = \frac{1}{2}$ in both settings. The case $p = x$ is addressed in detail in D'Amato and Zoli (2012).
16 The second-order conditions are easily shown to be always satisfied.
17 Assumptions made in the no Mafia case also ensure that second-order conditions are satisfied in the presence of the Mafia.
18 Recall that these costs amount to a fraction $1 - \alpha$ of total legal disposal costs.
19 We normalize fixed costs K to 0.
20 Our analysis does not account for the potentially disruptive costs of the Mafia under a social welfare point of view. See Garoupa (2000) and D'Amato and Zoli (2012) for a treatment of this issue.
21 Notice also that $V_s < \frac{1}{2} y \varepsilon (\alpha + 1)$.
22 Figure 5.1 (top) reports the case when $V < V_m < V_s$, where V_m and V_s are defined in the text and in the proof of Prop. 1.

23 In Figure 5.1 (bottom) it is assumed that $V > \hat{V} > V_s > V_m$, where
$\hat{V} = \dfrac{y\delta\varepsilon(\alpha+1)}{2(\delta+\varepsilon)}$.

References

Cecere, G., Mancinelli, S., and Mazzanti, M. 2013. 'Waste Prevention and Social Preferences: The Role of Intrinsic and Extrinsic Motivations'. Nota di Lavoro FEEM 44.

Choe, C. and Fraser, I. 1998. 'The Economics of Household Waste Management: A Review'. *Australian Journal of Agricultural and Resource Economics*, 42: 269–302.

D'Alisa, G., Burgalassi, D., Healy H., and Walter, M. 2010. 'Conflict in Campania: Waste Emergency or Crisis of Democracy' *Ecological Economics*, 70: 239–49.

D'Amato, A., Mazzanti, M., and Nicolli, F. 2011. 'Waste Sustainability, Environmental Policy and Mafia Rents: Analysing Geographical and Economic Dimensions'. CEIS Research Papers 213, University of Rome Tor Vergata.

D'Amato, A., Mazzanti, M., Nicolli, F., and Zoli, M. 2014. 'Illegal Waste Disposal, Territorial Enforcement and Policy. Evidence from Regional Data.' SEEDS Working Papers 3/2014.

D'Amato, A. and Zoli, M. 2012. 'Illegal Waste Disposal in the Time of the Mafia: A Tale of Enforcement and Social Well Being'. *Journal of Environmental Planning and Management*, 55: 637–55.

European Commission, DG Environment. 2000. *A Study on the Economic Valuation of Environmental Externalities from Landfill Disposal and Incineration of Waste.* Final Main Report Brussels: European Commission, DG Environment.

European Environment Agency (EEA). 2013. *Managing Municipal Solid Waste: A Review of Achievements in 32 European Countries.* Copenhagen: European Environment Agency.

Eurostat. 2013. News release, 33/2013, 4 March.

Ferrara, I. 2008. 'Waste Generation and Recycling'. *OECD Journal: General Papers*, 2008/2. http://dx.doi.org/10.1787/gen_papers-v2008-art10-en, accessed May 8, 2014.

Ferrara, I. and Missios, P. 2012. 'A Cross-Country Study of Household Waste Prevention and Recycling: Assessing the Effectiveness of Policy Instruments'. *Land Economics*, 88: 710–44.

Fullerton, D. and Kinnaman, T. C. 1995. 'Garbage, Recycling, and Illicit Burning or Dumping'. *Journal of Environmental Economics and Management*, 29: 78–91.

Fullerton, D. and Kinnaman, T. C. 2002. *The Economics of Household Garbage and Recycling Behaviour.* Cheltenham: Edward Elgar.

Garoupa, N. 2000. 'The Economics of Organized Crime and Optimal Law Enforcement'. *Economic Inquiry*, 38: 278–88.

Ham, Y. J., Maddison, D. J., and Elliott, R. J. 2013. 'The Valuation of Landfill Disamenities in Birmingham'. *Ecological Economics*, 85: 116–29.

Hoornweg, D. and Bhada-Tata, P. 2012. *What a Waste: A Global Review of Solid Waste Management*. Urban Development Series Knowledge Papers 15. Washington, DC: World Bank.

Legambiente. 2010. *Rapporto Ecomafie 2010*. Milano: Edizioni Ambiente.

Legambiente. 2011. *Rapporto Ecomafie 2011*. Milano: Edizioni Ambiente.

Legambiente. 2012. *Rapporto Ecomafie 2012*. Milano: Edizioni Ambiente.

Liddick, D. R. 2010. 'The Traffic in Garbage and Hazardous Wastes: An Overview'. *Trends in Organized Crime*, 13: 134–46.

Liddick, D. R. 2011. *Crimes Against Nature: Illegal Industries and the Global Environment*. Westport, CT: Praeger.

Massari, M. and Monzini, P. 2004. 'Dirty Business in Italy: A Case Study of Illegal Trafficking in Hazardous Waste'. *Global Crime*, 6: 285–304.

Organisation for Economic Co-operation and Development (OECD). 2008a. *OECD Environmental Data Compendium 2006–2008*. Paris: OECD Publishing.

Organisation for Economic Co-operation and Development (OECD). 2008b. *OECD Environmental Outlook to 2030*. Paris: OECD Publishing.

Pasotti, E. 2010. 'Sorting through the Trash: The Waste Management Crisis in Southern Italy'. *South European Society and Politics*, 15: 289–307.

Pearce, D. W. 2004. 'Does European Union Environmental Policy Pass a Cost–Benefit Test?' *World Economics*, 5: 115–38.

Porter, R. C. 2002. *The Economics of Waste*. Washington, DC: RFF.

Powell, J. C. and Brisson, I. 1994. 'The Assessment of Social Costs and Benefits of Waste Disposal'. CSERGE Working Paper WM 94–06.

Secretariat of the Basel Convention. 2012. *Vital Waste Graphics, 3*.

Tietenberg, T. and Lewis, L. 2012. *Environmental and Natural Resource Economics*, 9th edn. Harlow: Pearson.

Turner, G., Handley, D., Newcombe, J. and Ozdemiroglu E. 2004. 'Valuation of the External Costs and Benefits to Health and Environment of Waste Management Options'. Final Report for DEFRA by Enviros Consulting Limited in association with EFTEC. London: DEFRA. Available at: http://archive.defra.gov.uk/environment/waste/statistics/documents/costbenefit-valuation.pdf, accessed May 8, 2014.

6 Water conservation and management

Common sense for a common resource?

Simone Borghesi

Introduction

Water problems are receiving increasing attention in the political agenda of national governments and international institutions. The health and economic consequences of water scarcity and pollution have been provoking much concern among citizens who call for rapid solutions to these problems. To face the increasing water problems observed in most regions of the world, many governments have introduced a system of market incentives for water management and conservation and some countries have implemented market mechanisms based on tradable water pollution and consumption rights.

The use of market instruments is provoking a heated debate both among scholars and in the public opinion on two main issues: first, whether water should be treated as a common or a private good and, second, what is the most appropriate market instrument to apply the polluter (user) pays principle and thus price water pollution (consumption). The present chapter aims at analyzing these two issues and critically examine the experiences of various countries that have applied tradable water permit programs, highlighting the advantages and disadvantages that have emerged in each case, in order to provide useful indications for possible future applications in other regions. For this purpose, the chapter will first investigate the recent debate on water as a common resource and its practical implications in terms of water pricing, emphasizing the rationale and limitations underlying the use of market instruments for water. The chapter will then focus on tradable permits as this might become the main market instrument for water management and conservation to be adopted in many countries in the years to come. In this regard, the chapter critically evaluates the most significant applications of water tradable permit systems all over the world, focusing on the role that the government can play in their successful implementation, and provides a few suggestions which can be drawn from these programs for their application in other countries in the future.

For this purpose, the structure of the chapter is as follows. The next section discusses the ongoing debate on the nature of water as a common good and the conflicting opinions on water pricing that this has generated. The following section then examines selected experiences of application of water tradable permit systems, focusing on the importance of state intervention for the proper functioning of this market-based instrument. The final section provides some concluding remarks on the role that the government should play in water management and conservation to find a desirable equilibrium in the future between an increasing profit culture and an appropriate state culture.

Water as a common resource: the ongoing debate

Water scarcity and water pollution problems have been rapidly increasing in the last decades both in many arid regions and at the world level. Although in some cases water consumption habits were estimated to be fairly steady even over long time spells (see, for instance, Musolesi and Nosvelli 2009), water use grew at more than twice the demographic growth rate in the last century and water withdrawals are expected to keep on increasing by 50 per cent by 2025 in developing countries, and 18 per cent in developed countries (United Nations Environment Programme 2007).

Even if water resources were theoretically sufficient to meet the global demand, they are often insufficient to satisfy local demand. Transferring water resources across different locations (from places with an oversupply of water to places with water scarcity) requires huge investments that many developing countries cannot afford due to lack of financial resources. This often generates in these countries what can be defined as a poverty trap. The lack of water tends to lower the economic growth of the country; this generates in turn a lack of financial resources which prevents appropriate investments in the water sector, thus further worsening the water scarcity problem.

To get a deeper understanding of the current water consumption problems, in the last few years some scholars (Hoekstra and Chapagain 2008) have developed a new indicator, named the Human Water Footprint (HWF), which applies to water issues the notion of an ecological footprint originally introduced by Wackernagel and Rees (1996) by measuring humans' appropriation of freshwater resources. In this regard, Mekonnen and Hoekstra (2012) have shown that the HWF varies widely across countries and is deeply affected by different food consumption habits. In the US, for instance, the HWF of the average consumer is 2,842 m³/year, more than double the HWF of other huge countries like China (1,071 m³/year) and India (1,089 m³/year). Moreover, some food products that are largely consumed in Western countries need more water for their production than others. Thus, for instance, the consumption of cereal products gives the largest contribution (27 per cent) to the HWF of the average consumer, followed by meat (22 per cent) and milk products (7 per cent). It follows that several countries heavily rely on foreign water resources and have significant impacts on water consumption elsewhere.

Beyond water consumption problems, increasing water pollution problems have been observed worldwide. As is well known and well documented in the literature (see, among others, Schwarzenbach et al. 2010; WHO 2012, 2013) water pollutants cause severe health consequences that imply high social costs for the community. Just to provide a few examples and without being exhaustive, the presence in the water of heavy metals (lead, cadmium, mercury, arsenic, and nickel) and polluting chemical products (DDT, atrazine, dioxin, etc.) causes serious damage to the nervous system, liver, and kidneys and increases the risk of tumors by polluting soil, grain, vegetables, livestock, poultry, and fish products. Similarly, the concentration of fecal coliform bacteria in water where there is no efficient treatment is responsible for diarrhea, cholera, hepatitis and typhoid fever that account for about 88 per cent of total diseases among individuals aged under 15, particularly in the developing countries where 95 per cent of water is untreated. It has been estimated that more than 3.4 million deaths per year are due to diseases deriving from lack of safe water, sanitation and hygiene-related causes, and that 99 per cent of all deaths occur in developing countries (WHO 2008).

The water management problems briefly described above have generated a heated debate among both scholars and citizens on the very nature of water as a common resource. As is well known (cf. Ostrom and Ostrom 1977; Mankiw 2006), economists define a common good as being characterized by two features: non-excludability from consumption (individuals cannot be effectively excluded from its use) and rivalry in consumption (its use by one agent reduces availability to others).[1] Supporters of the common good viewpoint generally claim that none should be excluded from access to water. Water, in fact, is a basic need for the survival of any individual; therefore its accessibility represents a human right that should be guaranteed to everybody. This position was supported by the United Nations (UN) which in the General Assembly on July 28, 2010, through Resolution 64/292, formally acknowledged the human right to water and sanitation and declared that clean drinking water and sanitation are essential to the realization of all human rights (cf. UN-OHCHR et al. 2010). The UN, moreover, has explicitly recognized access for everybody to drinkable water and sanitation among its top priorities since the very first UN water conference in 1977 in Argentina. However, as some scholars have pointed out (e.g. Thielborger 2013; Francioni 2012), in international law a legally binding declaration either on human right to water or on water as a common good is still missing. In addition, although the target of giving everybody access to water and sanitation has been repeatedly renewed at all UN conferences through these years, we are still far from reaching it. In this regard, the target set by the Millennium Development Goals (halve by 2015 the number of people worldwide without access to safe water and sanitation services) appears difficult to meet as the deadline approaches. Although the world population with access to safe water increased from 73 per cent to 80 per cent during the 1990s, there are still 768 million people without access to safe water and 2.5 billion without access to sanitation facilities (WHO and UNICEF 2013).

The difficulty in providing everybody with proper access to water has generated an increasing public opinion movement across countries that puts pressure on national governments to recognize water as a common good (see, for instance, Shiva 2002, and the nine proposals therein cited for the "democratization of water" of the Community Environmental Bill of Rights). While none can deny the crucial role that water plays for our survival and hence its being in principle an inalienable human right, the existence of rivalry in consumption, the other main feature characterizing water as a common good, may prevent this theoretical right from being applicable in reality. Stated differently, one feature of the common good (rivalry in consumption) may clash with the other (non-excludability from consumption) and may lead people to be excluded from water consumption. In fact, if water consumption is not clearly regulated and properly limited ex ante, it may be impossible to allow everybody to have access to water resources. This has evidently emerged in many cases in which the lack of clearly defined property rights on water has led to overconsumption and possibly exhaustion of the resource, so that the desire to give everybody free access to water – if not properly limited – may end up giving nobody access to it. If we are to avoid its overexploitation and degradation, therefore, water must be given a price that induces environmentally friendly behaviors (i.e. a reduction of consumption and pollution). This pragmatic consideration suggests that the issue at stake is not whether water should be given a price, but rather how to price water and which price should be set. Giving water a price, in fact, does not imply that water management should be left completely to the market.

In this regard, there seem to be two opposite but equally detrimental misunderstandings of the water problem in large sections of public opinion. On the one hand, the inalienable right to water and the principle that water should be accessible to everybody does not mean that water should be free for all, as some opinion movements seem to conclude. If it were, an obvious and well-known free-riding problem would arise leading to the rapid exhaustion of the resource. On the other hand, the need to price water does not imply that an unregulated market should do it, as implicitly argued by the supporters of the neoliberal viewpoint. Both extreme positions should be rejected: the fact that the resource cannot be free does not mean that the market should be left completely free to price it. On the contrary, government intervention can help protect common goods that the market would not protect on its own. As shown by Cesi and Gorini in Chapter 2 of this book, the government can play a coordinating role that promotes the rise of cooperative equilibria that are needed to avoid free-riding problems.

The main challenge in the water puzzle, therefore, is to price water ensuring at the same time a truly competitive water market. Unfortunately, the current water market is far from competitive. A few large firms dominate the water market at the world level, thus leading to a substantially oligopolistic market structure. In fact, the four largest water multinationals (Veolia Environnement, Suez/Ondeo Environment, Saur Group, and Thames Water) jointly hold 95 per cent of the overall world water market managed by private societies. This has created much disillusion in public opinion on the actual capacity of the market to price water without generating distortions that lower social welfare and disparities among the agents.

One possible way out might involve the use of tradable permits as a suitable instrument to price water consumption and pollution. As is well known, in the case of water tradable permits a regulatory authority sets the water consumption (pollution) cap, that is, the maximum amount of water abstraction (pollution) allowed in the hydrographic basin, and allocates the corresponding abstraction (pollution) rights among the users of the basin who can then exchange them according to their present and/or future expected water consumption (pollution) needs. It follows that tradable permits may allow in the water context the operation of the consumer/polluter pays principle: consumers (polluters) who need to use (pollute) water more than allowed by the permits at disposal will have to purchase them on the market, thus incurring an additional cost for the negative externality that they provoke for the other agents.[2] Tradable permits, moreover, represent a sufficiently flexible instrument to allow for government intervention and correction. The regulatory authority, in fact, can appropriately modify the supply of water consumption/pollution rights according to the empirical evidence on the amount/quality of water in the hydrographic basin at stake. This intervention will obviously modify the price of the water tradable permits, in a similar vein to the money market operations performed by the central banks to influence the interest rate according to the available evidence on the situation of the money market.

To assess whether and to what extent these theoretical advantages of water tradable permits may be realized in practice, in what follows we will evaluate a few case studies in which they have been applied so far, with particular emphasis on the role played by the regulatory authority in implementing and affecting the efficacy of this instrument as well as on the capacity of the government to correct the problems that have arisen in specific contexts.

Water tradable permits and the role of the government: lessons learnt from application experiences

A few studies have recently tried to evaluate the application experience of water tradable permits around the world (Woodward et al. 2002; Woodward 2003; Kraemer et al. 2004; Borghesi 2013; Fisher-Vanden and Olmstead 2013). It is generally argued that tradable permits worked well in Australia and partly in the US, while they turned out to be nonactive or inefficient in most other countries and applications. While authors may have different views on specific aspects of these applications, there seems to be a large consensus on a few lessons that can be learnt from the case studies undertaken so far. An in-depth evaluation of all case studies goes beyond the scope of the present chapter (see Fisher-Vanden and Olmstead 2013 and Borghesi 2013 for recent, more exhaustive analyses in this regard). For this reason, we will focus here exclusively on how government intervention may affect the success/failure of such applications.

A major requirement for a successful system of water tradable permits is the capacity of the local government to monitor and regulate the market. This implies, in particular, its capacity to preserve and/or increase market competition. When market competition was insufficient due to the ability of larger firms to control most of the permits, the market remained inactive and no permits were exchanged. This applies, in particular, when the market is small and initially oligopolistic, like in the often-quoted case of the Fox River in Wisconsin (O'Neil et al. 1983; Hahn and Hester 1989) where the larger firms of the local cardboard and paper industry refused to sell their permits to the small firms to prevent their expansion and competitiveness. The opposite occurred in the application of tradable water rights on the Hunter River and the Murray-Darling Basin in Australia. The Australian Environmental Protection Agency managed to fix a telematic register and a system of online trading, monitored daily by a stakeholder committee (Kraemer et al. 2004) which enjoyed considerable success: the number of violations of the maximum limits decreased over time, while trading progressively extended both intra-state and inter-state.

Government policy can obviously influence market competitiveness not only directly through the attribution of water rights, but also indirectly through the allocation of subsidies and financial support to groups of agents. An emblematic example in this sense is provided by the case of several Southern Asian countries (e.g. Pakistan, Jordan, and Yemen) where water scarcity is particularly severe (Ahmad 2000; Almas and Scholz 2006). In all these countries water is extracted from the sources with electric or diesel pumps. The pump owners (normally the bigger farmers who can afford the installation costs for the machinery) generally extract as much water as possible before the others, with the aim to sell the excess amount on the market and thus recover the costs of the investment in the pump. The financial aid provided by the state to farmers to cover the electricity costs incurred by the pumps has worsened the depletion of the groundwater, reducing the cost of using a water pump and thus inducing many large farmers to extract more water than is actually needed.

Furthermore, these markets are frequently characterized by monopolistic structures which generate high prices, and result in higher costs for smaller farmers. In many small villages, only one farmer can afford to purchase a water extraction pump, therefore there will be only one holder who can sell these rights to the other smaller farmers in the village. It follows that the lack of competition between farmers on the product market (caused by the disparity of size and wealth between the farming firms and further worsened by the government subsidies to reduce the energy costs) ends up causing a lack of competition also on the water rights market.

The degree of uncertainty on the functioning of the market is another aspect that affects the success or failure of a water tradable permit scheme and that is heavily influenced by the government. In most successful programs the regulation authorities managed to reduce the agents' uncertainty. This applies, for instance, to the system of water pollution rights in California in which a state agency provided legal backing for vendors; this substantially lowered the legal risks deriving from the need to ensure that the counterpart respects the previously stipulated transaction rules (Garrido 1998). The opposite applies to those applications in which the existing uncertainty on different aspects of the system prevented agents from exchanging permits. In some developing countries, like Chile and Mexico for instance, some authors (e.g. Bauer 1997) argue that the allocation of water rights reflected political interests rather than transparent economic criteria. In contrast to California and Australia where the property rights and the trading rules have been clearly defined ex ante, in these countries agents suffer considerable uncertainty at the legal level since only part of the permits are officially registered with the competent authority, which might explain the small market activity observed on these markets (Bauer 1997; Bjornlund and McKay 2002).

As mentioned above, the possibility of modifying permit supply based on new evidence at disposal represents another important channel that the government has to influence the functioning of the water permits market. This channel, however, is not always easy to control. As a matter of fact, in several applications of tradable water pollution rights (e.g. Fox River in Wisconsin, Lake Dillon and Gulf of Cherry Creek in Colorado, the Valley of San Joaquin in California) the local authorities did not have enough information on the actual carrying capacity of the hydrographic basin as well as on the clean-up capacity of the polluting firms. This led the authorities to fix pollution limits that turned out to be either excessively severe (as in the Fox River) or excessively weak (as in the applications in Colorado and California mentioned above), which can explain the relative inactivity of these markets over the years (cf. Woodward et al. 2002; Fisher-Vanden and Olmstead 2013).

The lack of sufficiently accurate scientific information for the authority, therefore, may generate further uncertainty among the agents on the possible fluctuations in the permits' supply and, consequently, on the market price, which prevents the agents from intervening on the market.

While in principle the authorities could have performed fine-tuning policies by modifying the permits' supply according to their need, in reality this rarely occurred. In some cases (i.e. Colorado and California) the lack of government intervention could be ascribed to the pollution abatement performed by the firms that already had (or developed as a consequence) non-polluting technologies to avoid purchasing the pollution permits. In these cases, in fact, the lack of market transactions is not a problem as long as the very presence of a permit system induces the adoption of better technologies and, as a consequence, an improvement in water quality. In other cases, however, the lack of intervention and correction by the authority was probably due to a delay in the release of new scientific data on the actual pollution level, which tended to prevent and/or postpone the correcting measures that the authority should have adopted to deal with the problem.

Finally, an additional important driver underlying some successful applications of water permits is the involvement and active participation of the stakeholders. Even in this case, the government can play a crucial role in affecting the outcome of the market by promoting such participation. The evidence emerging from the existing applications tends to confirm this aspect. Some of the most successful systems of tradable permits (e.g. the pollution permits along the Hunter River and in the Tar-Pamlico Basin, or the consumption permits in the western states of the US) have seen the direct participation of the agents involved in the program. For example, in the Columbia Basin (that encompasses the US states of Oregon, Washington, Montana, and small portions of Nevada, Utah, and Wyoming), both federal governments and non-profit organizations have been largely involved in the design and implementation of market transactions, which have had promising environmental results in terms of the volume of water being restored (112 millions of cubic meters in 2007 alone, cf. Garrick et al. 2009). Similarly, in the Tar-Pamlico Basin half of the dischargers formed a voluntary association which cooperates with the state to develop a nutrient reduction strategy and an estuarine model for the basin (Jarvie and Solomon 1998). Such cooperation allows the regulator to know well in advance the possible concerns that may emerge on the program and meet them before proposing the program itself, so that the latter can already reflect the preferences of the agents involved. This suggests that support from public opinion represents an important prerequisite for the success of a program of this type. When the opposite happens, the market may be unable to "take off" even though the trading opportunities are potentially advantageous for the agents involved. This seemed to happen in Chile, for instance, where the community generally perceived the permits trading system as an external imposition from an ethical and cultural point of view. Most involved agents find it difficult to conceive that water abstraction rights for irrigating their crops can be separate from land ownership (Bauer 1997). This influences the individual reaction to the price signals and market incentives, and contributes in explaining why the only ones willing to sell their water rights are generally those who abandon agriculture to look for a job in the city centers, as they can no longer cover costs with the low income from farming. The comparison between the US applications and the Chilean case shows that cultural aspects and local traditions must be carefully taken into account when implementing tradable permits and that a "one-size-fits-all" design of such an instrument to be exported to different contexts does not exist.

This consideration raises a further question to be addressed when dealing with water problems. In those countries where market tradition and/or competition is low, can a collective and cooperative water management outperform the market? As emerges from the examples examined above, the market approach underlying the tradable permit system may be successful when the hydrographic basin involves large communities, so that the market size is sufficiently large. Moreover, a necessary condition for its proper functioning is that the market is competitive and sufficiently contestable, a condition that government intervention should try to ensure with appropriate policies whenever that is needed. In particular, the contestability of the permits market may play a crucial role for the active and successful involvement of the local community.

If the market is sufficiently contestable a water permit system enables stakeholders to enter the market and buy the rights in question, a viable option for those who use the water resources for recreation purposes, or for environmental groups who intend to safeguard the resource. By purchasing water permits, such groups can increase the permits' demand and price, thus compelling water consumers/polluters to pay more for their water consumption/pollution. In this way the permits can increase the stakeholders' capacity to influence the realization of economic policy objectives and speed up the transition towards environmentally friendly technologies.

But if stakeholders are not involved in the design of the permit system and if the market is not contestable (so that they cannot influence the price that is set by large oligopolistic firms) then cooperative management of water resources by the local community is probably preferable. The same also applies if the local community is small, so that the number of potentially interested participants is limited. In this case, no matter how active stakeholders may be, the market is unlikely to be sufficiently competitive and the number of transactions will be at most very limited, leading to a totally inactive market in a few years. If this is the case, the collective management of water resources can represent an alternative viable option for small local communities with little/no market competition underlying their economic structure.

In some Indian regions, for instance, the government often compensates local communities for the costs deriving from the collective management of natural resources. As Srigiri (2013: 91–3) points out, this tends to facilitate collective action as a strategy to achieve sustainability in watershed management, but the proper use of the inputs deriving from the government requires a sufficient amount of self-organization at different levels, such as self-help groups, user groups, as well as watershed associations and committees. The latter are particularly important as they supervise the implementation of plans proposed by user groups and self-help groups, and the enforcement of the rules of watershed management. As argued by Srigiri (2013: 119–20): "High levels of attendance in watershed committee meetings led to greater degree of consensus which further led to higher levels of voluntary labor contributions in communities." This suggests that the active participation of the involved stakeholders in the watershed committee plays a crucial role for the efficiency of collective action by the watershed community.

The Indian experience shows that if collaboration among immediate water users is sufficiently high and participation is not hindered by conflicts between upper and lower caste households so that everyone is motivated to attend the meetings, then "cooperation can be very effective in terms of making sustainable resource use feasible" (Hagedorn 2013:115).

Concluding remarks

The increasing consumption and pollution of water resources that we frequently observe today is the subject of heated debate in public opinion worldwide. In particular, much attention has been devoted to the dilemma concerning the very nature of water resources as common goods, and the legitimacy of their privatization. The idea that water, being an open access resource, should be free for everybody derives, in our opinion, from a misperception of the economic concept of a common resource: the rivalry in consumption that characterizes water resources requires water pricing if we are to avoid their overexploitation, therefore the fact that none should be excluded from consumption cannot be interpreted as meaning that water consumption should be free. The reasonable critique that is often made by certain opinion movements that water is a basic need for human subsistence and that poor people cannot afford to pay for it poses an important policy problem that the regulator should properly address, but does not eliminate the validity of the general principle that users/polluters should pay for their consumption/pollution. In the case of the poorest sector of the population, the principle can be applied by subsidizing their water consumption (within ecologically sustainable limits) through appropriate government redistribution policies. These policies, however, lead us back to the need to price water consumption. The real dilemma, therefore, is not whether water should be free, but rather how to price water properly.

In this regard, water tradable permits are gaining increasing attention from scholars and policy-makers as a suitable tool to apply the user (polluter) pays principle to water resources by creating an artificial market to price a common access resource that would otherwise be free and therefore subject to overexploitation and possible exhaustion. Like any other market, however, the market in water tradable permits is vulnerable and subject to a host of implementation problems when economic theory is confronted with practical application and everyday reality. The case studies that have been conducted so far and briefly described in this chapter suggest that water tradable permits work well when the local/central authority manages to monitor and regulate the market, reduce the uncertainty on the functioning of the instrument, ensure the competitiveness and contestability of the market, promptly modify permit supply according to new scientific evidence at disposal, and involve local stakeholders. But these requirements are not easily met due to pre-existing oligopolistic market structures that generate entry barriers, the lack of sufficient and reliable scientific information, or simply to the incapacity of the regulator to promptly intervene on the market for political/bureaucratic reasons and lack of support (or even opposition) from the involved stakeholders. All these factors that may hinder proper government intervention on the market can explain why several applications of water tradable permits have turned out to be unsuccessful, leading to markets that were basically inactive over several years.

While all the implementation problems described above can be equally detrimental for the functioning of the market, the application experiences suggest that a particularly relevant role is played by the lack of competition on the market for water tradable permits. Market failures such as environmental externalities require their internalization and tradable permits can provide the market-based instrument that is needed for this purpose. But if the markets for water tradable permits turn out to be non-competitive and/or non-contestable, we are led back into market problems. If this occurs, market-based instruments may tend to reproduce the problems that they were expected to solve. In this sense, it seems desirable to challenge people's uncritical faith in the market as the panacea for all problems (including water problems) and the related profit culture that has prevailed in the water context in the last decades and to encourage a state culture in water management and conservation. Although these remarks are purely common sense (as suggested by the somewhat provocative title of this chapter), they seem to be largely ignored by the supporters of the extreme neoliberal position (pro free market) on the water issue, as much as supporters of the opposite extreme view (pro free water) tend to ignore the unavoidable problems raised by keeping water as an open access resource.

The considerations presented above suggest that if we are to price water through market instruments, a proper and continuous government intervention is essential. However, if the hydrographic basin is too small to allow for sufficient market competition and/or if some of the above-mentioned factors prevent effective government monitoring and intervention, then alternative water management policies that involve active cooperation among local stakeholders should be considered as they can outperform market solutions. This seems to apply particularly in those developing countries in which the market tradition is weak and market creation can end up generating a very oligopolistic water market for tradable permits dominated by a few domestic firms and/ or large multinationals. In this regard, it may be important to enhance the role of local communities and look at the successful experience of "user group networks" in some developing countries as an alternative water management and conservation model with respect to traditional market-based instruments.

Notes

1 Individuals could in theory be excluded by the consumption of common goods, but in practice they are not, for social or technical reasons, thus leaving the goods as open access. It would, therefore, be more appropriate to talk about non-exclusion rather than non-excludability from consumption of the good. I am indebted to Stefano Gorini for pointing this out to me. While keeping this important distinction in mind, in what follows we will use the terminology commonly adopted in the literature (cf. Ostrom and Ostrom 1977; Tietenberg 2002; Mankiw 2006; Ostrom 2010) that classifies environmental resources in general and water resources in particular as common goods or common resources that – as Elinor Ostrom (2010) pointed out in her Nobel Prize lecture – share the attribute of rivalry of consumption (or subtractability as she calls it) with private goods and difficulty of exclusion with public goods.

2 As Massarutto (2011) points out, it is important to clarify the difference between water tradable permits and water privatization: by purchasing water consumption/pollution rights the consumer/polluter does not acquire the private property of the water resource, but rather a temporary right to use/pollute it that expires at the end of the permission period. Tietenberg (2002:197) claims that, when applied to the commons, tradable permits "do not privatize the resources, as conventional wisdom might suggest," but "they do privatize at least to some degree access to and use of those resources." The application of a system of water tradable permits, therefore, should not be confused with what is generally called water privatization, namely, the involvement of the private sector in the management of water services and/or the water infrastructures.

References

Ahmad, M. 2000. 'Water Pricing and Markets in the Near East: Policy Issues and Options'. *Water Policy*, 2(3): 229–42.

Almas, A. A. M. and Scholz, M. 2006. 'Agriculture and Water Resources Crisis in Yemen: Need for Sustainable Agriculture'. *Journal of Sustainable Agriculture*, 28(3): 55–75.

Bauer, C. J. 1997. 'Bringing Water Markets Down to Earth: The Political Economy of Water Rights in Chile, 1976–95'. *World Development*, 25(5): 639–56.

Bjornlund, H. and McKay, J. 2002. 'Aspects of Water Markets from Developing Countries: Experience from Australia, Chile and USA'. *Environment and Development Economics*, 7L 769–95.

Borghesi, S. 2013. 'Water Tradable Permits: A Review of Theoretical and Case Studies'. Forthcoming in *Journal of Environmental Planning and Management*.

Fisher-Vanden, K. and Olmstead, S. 2013. 'Moving Pollution Trading from Air to Water: Potential, Problems, and Prognosis'. *Journal of Economic Perspectives*, 27(1): 147–72.

Francioni, F. 2012. 'Realism, Utopia and the Future of International Environmental Law'. EUI Working Paper 2012/11. Department of Law, European University Institute, Florence.

Garrick, D., Siebentritt, M. A., Aylward, B., Bauer, C. J., and Purkey, A. 2009. 'Water Markets and Freshwater Ecosystem Services: Policy Reform and Implementation in the Columbia and Murray-Darling Basins'. *Ecological Economics*, 69: 366–39.

Garrido, A. 1998. 'Economics of Water Allocation and the Feasibility of Water Markets in Agriculture', in *Sustainable Management of Water in Agriculture: The Athens Workshop*. Paris: OECD, pp. 33–56.

Hagedorn, K. 2013. 'Natural Resource Management: The Role of Cooperative Institutions and Governance'. *Journal of Entrepreneurial and Organizational Diversity*, 2(1): 101–21.

Hahn, R. W. and Hester, G. L. 1989. 'Marketable Permits: Lessons from Theory and Practice'. *Ecology Law Quarterly*, 16(2): 361–406.

Hoekstra, A. Y. and Chapagain, A. K. 2008. *Globalization of Water: Sharing the Planet's Freshwater Resources*. Hoboken: Blackwell Publishing.

Jarvie, M. and Salomon, B. 1998. 'Point-Non Point Effluent Trading in Watersheds: A Review and Critique'. *Environmental Impact Assessment Review*, 18(2): 135–57.

Kraemer, A., Kampa, E., and Interwies, E. 2004. 'The Role of Tradable Permits in Water Pollution Control'. Working Paper. Washington, DC: Inter-American Development Bank.

Mankiw, G. 2006. *Principles of Microeconomics*. Mason, OH: South-Western.

Massarutto, A. 2011. *Privati dell'acqua? Tra bene comune e mercato*. Bologna: Il Mulino.

Mekonnen, M. M. and Hoekstra, A. Y. 2012. 'A Global Assessment of the Water Footprint of Farm Animal Products'. *Ecosystems*, 15(3): 401–15.

Musolesi, A. and Nosvelli, M. 2009. 'Water Consumption and Long-Run Socio-Economic Development: An Intervention and a Principal Component Analysis for the City of Milan'. *Environmental Modelling and Assessment*, 14(3): 303–14.

O'Neil, W., Martin, D., Moore, C., and Joeres, E. 1983. 'Transferable Discharge Permits and Economic Efficiency: The Fox River'. *Journal of Environmental Economics and Management*, 10(4): 346–55.

Ostrom, E. 2010. 'Beyond Markets and States: Polycentric Governance of Complex Economic Systems'. *American Economic Review*, 100(3): 641–72.

Ostrom, V. and Ostrom, E. 1977. 'Public Goods and Public Choices', in E. S. Savas (ed.), *Alternatives for Delivering Public Services: Toward Improved Performance*. Boulder, CO: Westview Press, pp. 7–49.

Schwarzenbach, R. P., Egli, T., Hofstetter, T. B., von Gunten, U., and Wehrli, B. 2010. 'Global Water Pollution and Human Health'. *Annual Review of Environment and Resources*, 35: 109–36.

Shiva V. 2002. *Water Wars: Privatization, Pollution, and Profit*. Cambridge, MA: South End Press.

Srigiri, S. R. 2013. 'Institutions of Collective Action and Property Rights for Natural Resource Management: Participation of Rural Households in Watershed Management Initiatives in Semi-Arid India'. *Institutional Change in Agriculture and Natural Resources*, 47. Aachen: Shaker.

Thielborger, P. 2013. *The Right(s) to Water: The Multi-Level Governance of a Unique Human Right*. New York: Springer.

Tietenberg, T. 2002. 'The Tradable Permits Approach to Protecting the Commons: What Have We Learned?' in E. Ostrom, T. Dietz, N. Dolsak, P. Stern, S. Stonich, and E. Weber (eds.), *The Drama of the Commons*. Washington, DC: National Academy Press, pp. 197–232.

United Nations Environment Programme. 2007. *Global Environment Outlook: Environment for Development (GEO-4)*. Malta: Progress Press.

United Nations, Office of the High Commissioner for Human Rights (UN-OHCHR), United Nations Human Settlements Programme (UN-Habitat), and World Health Organization (WHO). 2010. 'The Right to Water'. Fact Sheet 35. Geneva: United Nations.

Wackernagel, M. and Rees, W. 1996. *Our Ecological Footprint: Reducing Human Impact on the Earth*. Gabriola Island: New Society Publishers.

World Health Organization (WHO). 2008. *Safer Water, Better Health: Costs, Benefits, and Sustainability of Interventions to Protect and Promote Health*. Geneva: World Health Organization.

World Health Organization (WHO). 2012. *Global Costs and Benefits of Drinking-Water Supply and Sanitation Interventions to Reach the MDG Target and Universal Coverage*. Geneva: World Health Organization.

World Health Organization (WHO). 2013. *Water Quality and Health Strategy 2013–2020*. Geneva: World Health Organization.

World Health Organization (WHO) and UNICEF. 2013. *Progress on Sanitation and Drinking-Water – 2013 Update*. Geneva: World Health Organization.

Woodward, R. T. 2003. 'Lessons about Effluent Trading from a Single Trade'. *Review of Agricultural Economics*, 25(1): 235–45.

Woodward, R. T., Kaiser, R., and Aaron-Maire, W. 2002. 'The Structure and Practice of Water-Quality Trading Markets'. *Journal of the American Water Resources Association*, 38(4): 967–79.

7 Technological lock-in and the shaping of environmental policy

Annalisa Castelli

Introduction

The complexity of the technology/environment relationship is being increasingly debated, as industrial economies become aware of the carbon lock-in which is affecting their energy production choices. Consolidated theory has predicted that if competing technologies operate under dynamic increasing returns, one technology, even if an inferior one, will dominate the market. These results have been described referring to the fossil fuel-based technological system (Unruh 2000, 2002) or to the history of nuclear power technology (Cowan 1990). The mechanism itself is based on a set of technologies competing to dominate the market.

As clearly highlighted in previous chapters of this book, where areas of the real economy that strongly require active government intervention have been depicted, the issue of understanding whether to implement public policies intended to stimulate the choice of a particular technological path and, if yes, how to design these policies, is a crucial one. This strongly emerges observing the effects of well-intended but imperfectly designed environmental policies that, even if projected to mitigate, for example, carbon emissions, happen instead to increase them. The economic literature refers to this phenomena as the "Green Paradox" (Sinn 2008; Bhattacharyya 2011).[1] This concept should be clearly kept in mind when governments reason on policies intended to foster the adoption of a certain technology. These kinds of policies can lead the economy to be locked in to the chosen technology in the long run, implying increasing costs of change-over if, due to imperfect information, the chosen technology appears to be the "wrong" one.

With these concepts in mind this chapter is intended to deepen the issue of the choice of the optimal design of environmental policies and to reason on this optimality concept when the target of policy-makers is avoiding a socially harmful technology lock-in effect.

Moving from the seminal work of Arthur (1989) and drawing on Castelli et al. (2010) the main point here is that the well-established result according to which incentive-based instruments are to be preferred to the command and control ones, may be contradicted and even subverted when technology adoption should be somehow guided. The setting suggests a reason why environmental policy could be ill designed when the "chance" for lock-in to take place is overlooked, and draws attention to the importance of avoiding the dominance of a technology in presence of incomplete information.

A lock-in takes place when a technology, not necessarily the most efficient or the most green one, corners the market of potential adopters, due to technical as well as institutional increasing returns to scale (Liebowitz and Margolis 1995). As environmental policy affects the incentives to technology adoption, its design might have a role in determining lock-in.

It should be stressed here that, since governments are not able to perfectly discriminate among competing technologies in terms of their environmental impact, at least in the short run, the optimal choice available for them is, in most cases, to design environmental policies able to push forward the lock-in event.

Moving from these considerations and after reviewing several significant contributions from the literature on the issue, this work presents a very simple technology adoption model, trying to show that the desirability and opportunity of standard environmental and energy policy instruments in terms of technological development might change when lock-in phenomena are accounted for explicitly.

Background literature

Consolidated theory has predicted that if competing technologies operate under dynamic increasing returns, one technology, even if an inferior one, will dominate the market. These results have been described referring to the fossil fuel-based technological system (Unruh 2000, 2002) or to the history of nuclear power technology (Cowan 1990). The mechanism itself is based on a set of technologies competing to dominate the market. As clearly pointed out by Arthur (1989) we can observe increasing returns to adoption when the more a technology is adopted and the more experience is gained, the more the technology itself is improved. The event that led to the prevailing of one technology, by giving it the initial advantage in adoptions, can be completely insignificant by itself. After this random adoption in fact, the technology may improve more than others, also thanks to its diffusion, leading to a further widening of potential adopters. Thus a technology that became the leading one only by chance, can even "corner the market" of potential adopters locking out other competing technologies.

The most clear and well-known example of this mechanism is what happened when the QWERTY standard for keyboards became locked-in. Even if systems that were more efficient had been developed and could have been adopted, they have not been able to change the QWERTY standard, even when passing from typewriters to computers with nothing in the engineering of the latter that required that layout of letters.[2]

Competition among technologies can lead to many different outcomes, depending also on apparently insignificant events that can lead to a number of adopters that allow the technology to dominate the market and then to improve thanks to the leading position acquired. As economists know very well, allocation problems with increasing returns tend to exhibit multiple equilibria, and so it is not surprising that multiple outcomes should appear. Static analysis is able to locate these multiple equilibria but cannot say anything about the one that will be selected; dynamic approaches instead, by allowing the possibility of random events occurring during the adoption process, can better reveal how increasing returns might drive the adoption process into developing a technology that has inferior long-run potential (Arthur 1989).

The issue of the potential lock-in effect arising when adopting a new technology poses some questions. First, it is natural to try to understand if the economy is locked in a specific technology path and if this path is an inferior one.[3] Second, it should be useful to understand how to break out of locked-in technological standards.

This second question acquires great importance when wondering about costs and benefits arising to firms and consumers from the standardization of a product. It can happen in fact, when information is incomplete, that an industry could be trapped in an obsolete or inferior standard when there is a better alternative available.

There is more than one way in which consumers can benefit from standardization: a direct network externality, in the sense that one consumer's value for a good increases when another consumer has a compatible good (telephones, software); a market-mediated effect, as when a complementary good becomes cheaper and more widely available.

From the producer's point of view a kind of standardization will allow the firm to get inputs more cheaply by exploiting economies of scale in the production of those inputs. This kind of incentive does not necessarily correspond exactly to social benefits given that firms that benefit from compatibility or standardization could be reluctant to move to a new and better standard because of the coordination problem involved. The problem of coordinating innovation, or a change of standard, in an industry in which products not compatible with others are at substantial disadvantage, highlights an inefficient inertia, or inefficient innovation that cannot be completely resolved by communication among firms (Farrell and Saloner 1985).

The considerations above were intended to give the idea of relevant concepts when considering the introduction of a "general" innovation both in products than in processes.

The next section goes into the literature connected with the main point of this book, which is the choice of investing in "clean technologies."

Barriers to the adoption of clean technologies

Answering questions such as why the process of moving from an old technology to a "cleaner" one can be slow or may even not happen at all, requires one to reason on the fact that economic systems can be locked into previously adopted technological standards (Arthur 1989, 1990, 1994; Cowan 1990).

As described in the previous paragraph this kind of lock-in is due to increasing returns, deriving from a high number of users, and connected to the emerging of either economies of scale and of learning (Arrow 1962; Sheshinski 1967), network effects (Katz and Shapiro 1985, 1986; Farrell and Saloner 1985; Economides 1996), or the integrated and systemic nature of these technologies (Schilling 1998; Kemp 1996). The result is then a system with multiple equilibria that, as highlighted in David and Greenstein (1990), can be interpreted as a series of spontaneous standards. The exact interpretation of these standards acquires here a great importance; they are in fact the result of an internal market process and not of coordinated action of market participants. This means that the superiority of a technology with respect to another is not a guarantee of long-term sustainability (Cowan 1990; Nelson 1994) and that, in presence of increasing returns, designs that can seem inferior, can become locked in to the production system, in a historically dependent process in which circumstantial events determine the winning alternative (Carrillo-Hermosilla 2006).

The importance of the issue of a smart use of technologies is strengthened by the rapid broadening of environmental problems, by the uncertainty of their scale and duration, by their strong tendency towards irreversibility and by the growing social preference for environmental quality. This entails the necessity of finding the correct link between productive activity and environmental quality. This link lies obviously in technology, and it is necessary to understand how the process of technological change can lead towards sustainability (Carrillo-Hermosilla 2006).

There are a huge number of contributions reasoning on the consequences of the concept of technology lock-in in the environmental field. In the context of the so-called "evolutionary economics," for example, the works of Ayres (1991), Kemp and Soete (1992), Peters et al. (1999), Rammel and van den Bergh (2003), Kallis (2001), and Jaffe et al. (2000) deserve attention.

Scholars that study in the links between technological and ecological change, particularly in relation to the pollution externality from fossil fuel use, have developed interesting models (Kemp 1994; Rip and Kemp 1998; Unruh 2000). Kalkuhl et al. (2012), using an intertemporal general equilibrium model, show that small market imperfections may trigger a long-lasting dominance of an incumbent energy technology over a dynamically more efficient competitor, causing higher welfare losses than market failure alone.

Thinking about "conventional" instruments that can be used by governments and agencies in order to pursue their environmental goals one can cite economic and regulatory instruments that aim to control the negative impacts of production on the environment ex post. These policies have mainly led to incremental changes in the established technologies which, considering the progressive deterioration of the environment, are not sufficient.

The strong necessity of a more sustainable economic system requires fundamental changes in the technology regime, particularly in those sectors with a great environmental impact (Mulder et al. 1999; Freeman 1996; Arentsen et al. 1999).

Again, as noted by Carrillo-Hermosilla (2006), many authors admit that it is relatively unlikely that conventional environmental policy measures, not necessarily focused on technological change, may alone be able to bring about this radical change in technologies and practices. Among them are Belis-Bergouignan et al. (2004), Kline (2001), Smith (2000), Kuper and Van Soest (1999), and Carraro and Siniscalco (1994).

These considerations raise the important issue on whether it would be advisable to undertake policies purposely aimed at the sustainable technological change, applying an ex ante approach in a way that is complementary to the conventional equilibrium oriented environmental policies (Carrillo-Hermosilla 2006). Under this perspective, the need of a sustainable technological change requires policy-makers to face the challenge of preventing lock-in phenomena.

Although the literature shows that the transition among different equilibria can be spontaneous, the problem lies in the timing and direction of this transition that could be, sometimes, socially inappropriate in opening space for public intervention. The factor that fosters public intervention in case of a process of technology diffusion with increasing returns to adoption, lies in the supposed greater ability of the government to coordinate technology choices when trying to achieve environmentally superior timing. In other words, it seems that a coordination mechanism to guide the process of technological change towards the path of sustainability, could be desirable.

On this line of reasoning, Aklin and Urpelainen (2013) find out that political competition modifies the effect of path dependence on environmental policies. While "green governments" can use positive reinforcement mechanisms to lock in policy commitments, "brown" governments strategically underprovide public support to renewable energies.

Carrillo and Hermosilla (2006) propose a novel taxonomy of technological and environmental policies, for prevention rather than for transition, that builds on an evolutionary view of technological change and sustainable development, and permits a more formal justification of the appropriateness to new sustainability problems of the various instruments available in practice.

Policy instruments

This section is intended to draw a picture of instruments available to policy-makers who want to foster the adoption of clean technologies, without deepening too much the huge literature concerning the debate between economic incentives and command and control instruments.

The choice that policy-makers face when seeking to solve environmental problems derives from the answers they give to questions such as: whether taxing polluters for their discharges could be more effective than fining them when their level does not meet certain emissions standards; whether it is less costly for a regulatory agency to enforce a ban or to design a system of tradable permits; which strategy could be the best to reduce a pollutant in the most efficient way. Factors that should be considered to decide which is the "best" policy to pursue, can lead to the use of economic incentives or to the use of direct regulation (command and control instruments). These factors could be, for example, the regulatory infrastructure of a country or the nature of the environmental problem to be tackled.

Harrington and Morgenstern (2004) compared economic incentives and command and control policies and their outcomes in a real-world setting focusing on the United States compared to a set of European countries. This allowed the authors to consider six different environmental problems that the country observed dealt with differently, meaning that they used either economic incentives or command and control policies.[4] Results show that most policies had at least some elements of both approaches but they have been categorized into the two groups based on their dominant features. Looking at their outcomes it appears clear that economic incentives instruments produce cost savings in pollution abatement, as well as innovations that reduce the overall cost. It should be highlighted, however, that the finding about economic incentives' economic efficiency is tempered by the evidence that polluting firms prefer a command and control instrument because of its perceived lower cost.

From a historical perspective, Harrington and Morgenstern work highlights that in the 1970s almost all environmental policies relied on direct regulation, with very rare instances of economic incentives instruments, while during the late 1980s, whenever a new policy was proposed, policy-makers at least considered, and often selected, an economic incentives instrument. That said, almost all the policies studied by the authors are a blend of both, beginning as a command and control policy and then having economic incentives elements added or substituted.

The main reason why Harrington and Morgenstern's (2004) study is relevant for this work is that it reports the significant environmental results of the policies. Emissions fell by about two-thirds when compared to baseline estimates with most outcomes either meeting or exceeding policy-makers' original expectations.

Even if these are the results of a case study, generally speaking it is worthwhile to note that during the 1980s there was a great reliance on regulations represented by standards and controls. During the 1990s instead, there was a big "global environmental crises" that highlighted some practical limits of command and control regulation. The main point is that the use of this kind of regulation has demonstrated that its effect can be limited, and sometimes can become negative, if it is not accompanied by changes in economic and fiscal policies providing positive incentives for environmentally sound and sustainable economic development (Conrad and Wang 1993).

The design and the introduction of emissions taxes, both at the global then at the local level, should be carefully projected because such a price instrument is likely to affect all industries, whatever their individual size and their choice of the optimal number of plants. This means that dealing carefully with the economic impact of an emissions tax or of a subsidy for abated emissions on the structure of the economy requires a general equilibrium analysis. If the structure of the economy is perfectly competitive, Baumol and Oates (1988) showed that a Pigouvian tax will induce Pareto-optimal exit and entry decisions by all competitive firms. On the other side, Mestelman (1982) examined the effects of taxes and subsidies in a competitive economy using a general equilibrium model. His reasoning, based on the form of the subsidy described by Baumol and Oates, indicates that the use of the subsidy itself is inefficient. Depending on the market structure, firms' reactions to the introduction of a subsidy might be different and therefore might have a different effect on prices, output, entry, and exit. If this is the case, then an environmental policy has to take into account those differences in response in order to minimize distortions and deadweight losses (Conrad and Wang 1993).

As is clear from the above, the economic analysis of environmental problems has relied on increasingly sophisticated models of the interaction among sectors. For example, Ballard and Medema (1993) use a Computational General Equilibrium model (CGE) on the US tax system, in which certain types of pollution externality are included explicitly, looking at the efficiency effects of taxes and subsidies in the presence of such externalities. Their work deals with the interactions among fiscal instruments, environmental pollution, and the productive economy, as well as with the effects of substituting the Pigouvian tax or subsidy with an increase or decrease in the labor income tax. Results demonstrate that a Pigouvian tax may be preferred, both as a revenue source than as a method of externality correction.

The setting

Using Arthur (1989) as a reference, this section aims to investigate how different environmental policy instruments might be effective or not in influencing the chance for an economy to become locked in on an unsustainable path.

Considering two technologies S and U which, for now, cannot be distinguished in terms of best or worst environmental impact, and assuming two types of agents, G and Q, again identical for now, that have to choose which technology to adopt, the framework is the following:

Agent i comes to the market in time t_i, chooses to adopt one of the two technologies and uses the adopted technology thereafter. In other words, at each point in time one agent gets to the market and chooses, once and forever, the technology he wants to adopt and use. We assume that the chance for each agent type to get to the market in each point in time is one half; roughly speaking, the number of agents of each type is the same. Agents differ in terms of the benefits they get from adopting the two technologies.

The payoff function for agent G by adopting technology S is as follows:

$$s_G + gn_S \tag{1}$$

while the corresponding payoff from technology U is

$$u_G + gn_U \tag{2}$$

implying that the adoption of technology j *($j = S;U$)* depends on positive values sG and uG as well as on how many agents have already adopted the technology, according to the positive parameter g.

This is the most simplified way of modeling network externalities and/or increasing returns. The corresponding benefit functions for type Q agents are:

$$S_Q + qn_S \tag{3}$$

if they adopt technology S and

$$u_Q + qn_U \tag{4}$$

if they adopt technology U. As previously, q is a positive parameter playing the same role as g for G-type agents. Considering the assumption, without loss of generality, that agents G have a "natural preference" for technology S while agents Q prefer technology U, it implies assuming that $sG > uG$ and that $sQ < uQ$.

The indeterminacy in the adoption process is introduced by the assumption that there is a social planner or an environmental regulator that can observe the sequence of agents choosing their preferred technology, but has no knowledge about the "historical events" (political and rent-seeking behavior, experience of adopters, etc.) responsible for the sequence by which the agents make their choice. In other words the hypothesis here is that, at the moment in which the technology is adopted, and the government chooses a specific policy, no one is able to know what is the difference among competing technologies in terms of their environmental expected impact.

Everything about demand (i.e. agents, preferences) and supply (one unit of each technology is inelastically supplied at each point in time) is instead common knowledge.

Experiencing lock-in

Given the assumptions so far, we can still follow Arthur (1989) and define the difference in adoption as the difference in the number of agents that adopted the new technology once n agents have made their own choice, that is:

$$d_n = n_S(n) - n_U(n) \tag{5}$$

Under the assumption of increasing returns, we can distinguish two circumstances concerning adoption incentives by the two agent types.

(a) when the number of adopters is relatively low, then it is likely that G agents will choose technology S and Q agents will choose technology U. In other words, when increasing returns are not significant, the "natural ordering" of preferences is maintained;

(b) when a considerable number of agents have adopted a certain technology, then lock-in might occur. Consider the case in which the number of adopters of technology U is so high that also agents G, though having a "natural" preference for technology S, turn their choice to technology U. This happens when:

$$d_n = n_S - n_U < \Delta_U = \frac{u_G - s_G}{g} \tag{6}$$

which means saying that when the above condition is satisfied, then all agents will choose technology U, so that the economy will be locked in. Following the same reasoning, it can be shown that the economy would be locked into technology S when the following condition holds:

$$d_n = n_S - n_U > \Delta_S = \frac{u_Q - s_Q}{q} \tag{7}$$

Roughly speaking, when increasing returns are present, if the number of adopters of one technology is so high to make it worthwhile for all agents to choose that technology, then the economy will be locked in. The two threshold levels are represented in Figure 7.1.

Environment and the lock-in effect: how to avoid or delay it?

Having sketched the reference setting we can now try to understand if and how an environmental regulator can avoid the lock-in effect, or at least choose a strategy able to delay its effects. The idea is to compare the functioning of an incentive based instrument, such as a

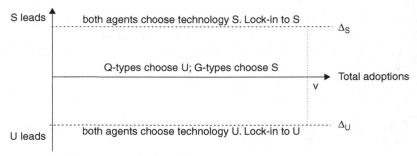

Figure 7.1   Possible lock-in thresholds

green tax/subsidy, with a command and control instrument, such as a technology ban.

Before going into details it is important to stress that the tax rates we have in mind here necessarily differ from the rates implied by the Pigouvian principle, according to which the optimal tax rate equals the marginal environmental damages. This also relies on results such as Bovenberg and Goulder (1996) that allow the possibility of an optimal tax rate that can be less than the rate supported by the Pigouvian principle. Moreover, and as highlighted in other parts of this work, the model here presented is an abstract way of looking at a specific case. In the rest of the work, whenever we will talk about green taxes we will have in mind a "general" concept of the instrument that applies differently to the agent depending on the chosen technology; we will then call the incentive based instrument a "green tax." A negative value for such tax will indeed represent a subsidy.

At the start, we assume that the lock-in has not taken place yet and that the environmental regulator has a given budget (so that it cannot provide unlimited subsidies) and a finite taxing power (so that it cannot impose unreasonably high taxes). The problem for the environmental regulator is therefore to choose the proper instrument to avoid the economy being locked into an unsustainable path.

We model the consequences of a command and control policy (i.e. a technology ban) on net benefits from technology adoption by assuming that some of the benefits are lost by the two agents due to compliance costs. In other words α and β represent the simplest way we can use to take care of compliance costs. It is important to stress here that these parameters model compliance costs and their reciprocal relationship in the most abstract way available, just allowing them to differ between each other. This is because, given that the main interest of this exercise is to study the effects of different environmental policies in delaying lock-in as much as possible, we implicitly assume that the benefits deriving from the two different adoptions are identical.

Under a technology ban the net benefits are as follows:

$$\alpha s_G + gn_S \tag{8}$$
$$\alpha u_G + gn_U$$

for type G and

$$\alpha s_Q + qn_S \tag{9}$$
$$\alpha u_{GQ} + gn_U$$

for type Q; where $\alpha < 1$ implies that net benefits are "scaled down" due to the ban. Under a green tax the net benefits from technology adoption are:

$$\beta s_G + gn_S - t_S \tag{10}$$
$$\beta u_G + gn_U - t_U$$

for type G and

$$\beta s_Q + qn_S - t_S \tag{11}$$
$$\beta u_Q + qn_U - t_U$$

for type Q; where $\beta < 1$, again, represents lost benefits due to compliance costs while t_U and t_S are the amount of levy on each technology. Notice that we allow for "green" taxation on both technologies because we want to account for the case where the regulator does not know which technology is the sustainable one.

The consequences of a technology ban are straightforward: it locks the economy in the unbanned technology.[5]

Under a green tax, conditions (6) and (7) become:

$$d_n < \Delta_U^t = \beta \frac{u_G - s_G}{g} - \frac{t_U - t_S}{g} \tag{12}$$

$$d_n > \Delta_S^t = \beta \frac{u_Q - s_Q}{q} - \frac{t_U - t_S}{q} \tag{13}$$

As a consequence, given that $\beta < 1$ and that we have assumed $sG > uG$ and $sQ < uQ$, then:

(a)   when $t_U > t_S$ then $\Delta'_S < \Delta_S$ while $\Delta'_U - \Delta_U$ is determined by the relative relevance of β and the tax differential;

b)   when $t_U < t_S$ then $\Delta'_U < \Delta_U$, while $\Delta'_S - \Delta_S$ is determined by the relative relevance of β and the tax differential.

In general, the effect of the green tax on the above thresholds will be determined by the complex interaction among:

1.   the degree of increasing returns of the two technologies;
2.   the difference in the two tax levies;
3.   the compliance cost parameter (i.e. β).

The height of the "no lock-in" band is given by

$$\Delta'_S - \Delta'_U = \beta \left(\frac{u_Q - s_Q}{q} - \frac{u_G - s_G}{g} \right) - \left(t_U - t_S \right) \frac{g - q}{gq} \tag{14}$$

We can, therefore, have two cases:

(a)   when increasing returns are greater for technology S ($g > q$); then the no lock-in band will be narrower if $t_U > t_S$ while it can be wider only if $t_U - t_S < 0$ and sufficiently large in absolute value.

(b)   when increasing returns are smaller for technology S ($g < q$); then the no lock-in band will be narrower if $t_U < t_S$ while it can be wider only if $t_U - t_S > 0$ and sufficiently large in absolute value.

All this considered, the problem lies in the fact that it is not certain that the regulator has complete information; it can happen in fact that he does not know for sure which is the sustainable technology. As a consequence we should reason on two different scenarios:

Scenario 1: the sustainable technology is known

Assume that at some point in time the environmental regulator has acquired perfect knowledge about the socially optimal technology. Suppose that technology U is the "bad" (Unsustainable) technology, while S is the "good" (Sustainable) technology. According to Arthur (1989) and which we have explained so far, as the number of adopters (n) increases, then the probability that lock-in takes place goes to one.

As a consequence, in an increasing returns setting, we know that the economy will be, sooner or later, locked in.

As already discussed, an incentive based policy, such as a green tax, would have the effect of shifting the lock-in threshold as well as changing the no lock-in ban height. This would, however, just change the timing and potential kind of lock-in, but it would not guarantee that the danger of being locked in the use of technology U is avoided. This conclusion is even stronger if the tax introduced is not a permanent one but only temporary.

The tax suffers, in this respect, from another shortcoming. Suppose that technology S is not taxed, as it is reasonable. The tax (amount) needed to avoid lock-in would have to be, in this case, such that:

$$t_U > (u_G - s_G) - gd_n \tag{15}$$

for a negative value of dn; given a weak preference for sustainable technology and significant increasing returns to the sustainable technology, the levy could be so high as to exceed government taxing power. In such a case, the required incentive based instrument would become unfeasible.

Turning to the command and control policy example, a ban on technology U at a certain time would simply imply that onward all agents would be forced to choose the other technology. Of course, such a ban could encounter strong resistance from the most affected agents (Q-type agents) so that not all the feasibility problems would be solved. On the other hand, a permanent technology ban would be the only instrument capable of guaranteeing that the economy is not locked in along a path where the "bad" technology is chosen by all agents.

Scenario 2: the sustainable technology is unknown

When the regulator does not have any knowledge concerning which technology is sustainable and which is not, a green tax can be an appealing instrument choice, as it allows to forward the lock-in effect and in so doing governments have more time to learn which technology is the sustainable one. In this case, a technology ban would have the strong disadvantage of locking the economy in the unsustainable technology with probability one half.

To give an example of the working of our setting, suppose that technology S is indeed the sustainable one, but government does not know this. Assume, further, that increasing returns are greater for the unsustainable technology, so that $q > g$. This means, in terms of Figure 7.2

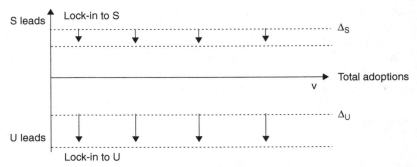

Figure 7.2   The widening of the 'no lock-in band'

that, assuming $t_U > t_S$ and sufficiently large, the no lock-in band becomes wider. As a consequence, the event of being locked in is somehow postponed.

Our analysis so far suggests that a tax could indeed be preferable to a standard when the environmental regulator does not have sufficient information to choose which technology must be favored.

A clear policy implication stems from our sketched results, namely, the need for a timely "combination" of instruments. Since, in general, governments do not know which one is the sustainable technology, by introducing a tax in the early stages of technology adoption, they would avoid lock-in and gain time for learning; afterwards, when the sustainability implications of the competing technologies become clearer, governments could switch to command and control in terms of a ban on the "bad" technology.

Although the desirability of a green tax and the switching time among instruments are only qualitative conclusions, as they depend on factors which are not explicitly modeled in our simplified setting, namely the government learning process and the a priori probability distribution among technologies, they can in any case represent an important signal for the government.

When the main concern is to avoid, or to delay as much as possible, technological lock-in, to which future increasing welfare losses are associated, and there is uncertainty about the sustainable technology, then to resort to a temporary green tax may be the best solution.

Conclusions

This work has reviewed some of the literature on lock-in effects and environmental policies and, building on the seminal paper by Arthur

(1989) and on the theory of environmental policy instruments, has tried to include lock-in considerations into the choice that governments face when projecting their environmental policies.

Our findings highlight additional considerations concerning the relative desirability of a blending of command and control and incentive based instruments.

Although these are very preliminary results strongly limited by the choice of a simplified model in which we do not allow for differences in agents, costs, and technologies effects, and employ a general concept of green taxes, so as to strongly focus only on the effects of different policies, we think that they represent a first step in opening the black box of optimal environmental policies design when technology adoption is a concern.

Based on the theory of lock-in under increasing returns, we discover some promising insights in support of the conclusion that the standard environmental policy approach is not enough when long-run properties of policy instruments are the main concern. Indeed, including lock-in considerations into the analysis can subvert "traditional" conclusions, suggesting that command and control policies may be the only available instrument to ensure the economy is not locked into an unsustainable technology, or at least allowing the lock-in effect to be delayed so as to gain more time to learn about competing technologies. The policy suggestion that stems from our sketched results points, so far, to the need for a timely combination of instruments.

Notes

1 For a detailed reasoning on the Green Paradox phenomena see Chapter 4 of this volume.
2 For a full description of the QWERTY adoption process, see David (1985).
3 Examples could be the adoption of the alternating current (Bunn and David 1987), the US color television system, or the programming language FORTRAN.
4 The European countries considered are: France, Germany, the Netherlands, Norway and Sweden.
5 We assume that once the ban has been introduced it cannot be easily removed. In other words, the ban is assumed to be in place for enough time to generate lock-in.

References

Aklin, M. and Urpelainen, J. 2013. 'Political Competition, Path Dependence, and the Strategy of Sustainable Energy Transitions'. *American Journal of Political Science*, 57(3): 643–58.

Arentsen, M. J., Dinica, V., and Marquart, E. 1999. 'Innovating Innovation Policy: Rethinking Green Innovation Policy in Evolutionary Perspective'.

Communication to the European Meeting on Applied Evolutionary Economics, June 7–9, Grenoble, France.

Arrow, K. J. 1962. 'The Economic Implications of Learning by Doing'. *Review of Economic Studies*, 29(3): 155–73.

Arthur, W. B. 1989. 'Competing Technologies, Increasing Returns and Lock-In by Historical Events'. *Economic Journal*, 99: 116–31.

Arthur, W. B. 1990. 'Positive Feedbacks in the Economy'. *Scientific American*, February: 92–9.

Arthur, W. B. 1994. *Increasing Returns and Path Dependence in the Economy*. Ann Arbor: University of Michigan Press.

Ayres, R. U. 1991. 'Evolutionary Economics and Environmental Imperatives'. *Structural Change and Economic Dynamics*, 2: 255–73.

Ballard, C. L. and Medema, S. G. 1993. 'The Marginal Efficiency Effects of Taxes and Subsidies in the Presence of Externalities'. *Journal of Public Economics*, 52: 199–216.

Baumol, W. J. and Oates, W. E. 1988. *The Theory of Environmental Policy*, 2nd edition. Cambridge: Cambridge University Press.

Belis-Bergouignan, M. C., Oltra, V., and Saint Jean, M. 2004. 'Trajectories towards Clean Technology: Example of Volatile Organic Compound Emission Reductions'. *Ecological Economics*, 48: 201–20.

Bhattacharyya, S. C. 2011. *Energy Economics: Concepts, Issues, Markets and Governance*. London: Springer.

Bovenberg, A. L. and Goulder, L. H. 1996. 'Optimal Environmental Taxation in the Presence of Other Taxes: General Equilibrium Analyses'. *American Economic Review*, 86(4): 985–1006.

Bunn, J. and David, P. A. 1987. 'The Economics of Gateway Technologies and Network Evolution: Lessons from Electricity Supply History'. Paper 119. Centre for Economic Policy Research, Stanford.

Carraro, C. and Siniscalco, D. 1994. 'Environmental Policy Reconsidered: The Role of Technological Innovation'. *European Economic Review*, 38: 545–54.

Carrillo-Hermosilla, J. 2006. 'A Policy Approach to the Environmental Impacts of Technological Lock-In'. *Ecological Economics*, 58: 717–42.

Castelli, A., Castellucci, L., and D'Amato, A. 2010. 'Do Lock-In Considerations Affect Environmental Policy Instrument Choice?' Paper presented at the Fourth World Congress of Environmental and Resources Economists (WCERE), Montreal, June.

Conrad, K. and Wang, J. 1993. 'The Effects of Emission Taxes and Abatement Subsidies on Market Structure'. *International Journal of Industrial Organization*, 11: 499–518.

Cowan, R. 1990. 'Nuclear Power Reactors: A Study in Technological Lock In'. *Journal of Economic History*, 50(3): 541–67.

David, P. A. 1985. 'Clio and the Economics of QWERTY'. *American Economic Review*, 75(2): 332–7.

David, P. A. and Greenstein, S. 1990. 'The Economics of Compatibility Standards: An Introduction to Recent Research'. *Economics of Innovation and New Technology*, 1(1–2): 3–41.

Economides, N. 1996. 'The Economics of Networks'. *International Journal of Industrial Organization*, 14(6): 673–99.

Farrell, J. and Saloner, G. 1985. 'Standardization, Compatibility and Innovation'. *Rand Journal of Economics*, 16: 70–83.

Freeman, C. 1996. 'The Greening of Technology and Models of Innovation'. *Technological Forecasting & Social Change*, 53: 27–39.

Harrington, W. and Morgenstern, R. D. 2004. 'Economic Incentives versus Command and Control: What Is the Best Approach to Solve Environmental Problems?' Rff Discussion Paper 152.

Jaffe, A. B., Newell, R. G., and Stavins, R. N. 2000. 'Technological Change and the Environment'. *Discussion Paper vol. 00–47, Resources for the Future*, Washington, DC.

Kalkuhl, M., Edenhofer, O., and Lessmann, K. 2012. 'Learning or Lock-In: Optimal Technology Policies to Support Mitigation'. *Resource and Energy Economis*, 34: 1–23.

Kallis, G. 2001. 'A Co-Evolutionary Institutional Approach to Sustainable Development: Theory and Potential Applications'. *Frontiers I Conference ESEE*, Cambridge, UK, July 3–7.

Katz, M. L. and Shapiro, C. 1985. 'Network Externalities, Competition and Compatibility'. *American Economic Review*, 75(3): 424–40.

Katz, M. L. and Shapiro, C. 1986. 'Technology Adoption in the Presence of Network Externalities'. *Journal of Political Economy*, 94(4): 822–41.

Kemp, R. 1994. 'Technology and the Transition to Environmental Sustainability'. *Futures*, 26(10): 1023–46.

Kemp, R. 1996. 'The Transition from Hydrocarbons: The Issues for Policy', in S. Facheux, D. Pearce, and J. Proops (eds.), *Models of Sustainable Development*. Cheltenham: Edward Elgar, pp. 151–75.

Kemp, R. and Soete, L. 1992. 'The Greening of Technological Progress: An Evolutionary Perspective'. *Futures*, June: 437–55.

Kline, D. 2001. 'Positive Feedback, Lock-In, and Environmental Policy'. *Policy Sciences*, 34: 95–107.

Kuper, G. H. and Van Soest, D. P. 1999. 'Asymmetric Adaptations to Energy Price Changes: An Analysis of Substitutability and Technological Progress in the Dutch Economy'. Paper presented at PRET Workshop, Maastricht, March 18–19.

Liebowitz, S. and Margolis, S. E. 1995. 'Path Dependence, Lock-In and History'. *Journal of Law, Economics and Organization*, 11(1): 205–26.

Mestelman, S. 1982. 'Production Externalities and Corrective Subsidies: A General Equilibrium Analysis'. *Journal of Environmental Economics and Management*, 9: 186–93.

Mulder, P., Reschke, C. H., and Kemp, R. 1999. 'Evolutionary Theorizing on Technological Change and Sustainable Development'. European Meeting on Applied Evolutionary Economics, Grenoble, France, June 7–9.

Nelson, R. R. 1994. 'The Coevolution of Technologies and Institutions', in R. W. England (ed.), *Evolutionary Concepts in Contemporary Economics*. Ann Arbor: University of Michigan Press, pp. 139–56.

Peters, I., Ackerman, F., and Bernow, S. 1999. 'Economic Theory and Climate Change Policy'. *Energy Policy*, 27(9): 501–4.

Rammel, C. and Van den Bergh, J. C. J. M. 2003. 'Evolutionary Policies for Sustainable Development: Adaptive Flexibility and Risk Minimizing'. *Ecological Economics* 47: 121–33.

Rip, A. and Kemp, R. 1998. 'Technological Change', in S. Rayner and E. L. Malone (eds.), *Human Choice and Climate Change: Resources and Technology.* Columbus: Battelle Press, pp. 327–99.

Schilling, M. A. 1998. 'Technology Lockout: An Integrative Model of the Economic and Strategic Factors Driving Technology Success and Failure'. *Academy of Management Review* 23(2): 267–84.

Sheshinski, E. 1967. 'Tests of the Learning by Doing Hypothesis'. *Review of Economics and Statisics*, 49(4): 568–78.

Sinn, H. W. 2008. 'Public Policy against Global Warming: A Supply Side Approach'. *International Tax and Public Finance*, 15: 360–94.

Smith, K. 2000. 'Innovation as a Systemic Phenomenon: Rethinking the Role of Policy'. *Enterprise and Innovation Management Studies*, 1(1): 73–102.

Unruh, G. C. 2000. 'Understanding Carbon Lock In'. *Energy Policy*, 28: 817–30.

Unruh, G. C. 2002. 'Escaping Carbon Lock In'. *Energy Policy*, 30: 317–25.

8 Common land resources and forests

The role of (multi-level) governance

Amanda Spisto

The current discussion about common pool resources

Conventional theory on common pool resources (CPRs) predicts that, under specific basic theoretical assumptions, overharvesting and depletion of the resource will result. The problems that resource users face in managing CPRs are strictly concerned with appropriation and other forms of social and economic interdependencies present in natural settings (Ostrom et al. 1999).

Access to the resources is free and not regulated. At the same time CPRs, like forests, own specific features of private good, in the sense that to a certain extent their appropriation is excludable and rival when, because of their unsustainable harvesting, users deplete the resource stock available to others (negative externality).

As emphasized by Gardner et al. (1990) there exists additional complexity around CPRs related to the provision activities engaged by local users. A number of examples in which appropriation and provision activities are linked together can be found in field studies examining the local governance of rice farming and fishing communities (Berkes et al. 1989), groundwater users (Chomitz et al. 2006), and grazing in forest-dependent communities (Agarwal and Singh 1992).

The appropriators face behavioral incentives in contributing towards provision activities that benefit the entire community. For example, farmers who jointly use an irrigation system organize a number of provision activities such as in-kind maintenance of the system (e.g. repairing irrigation ditches) or construction of structures to trap or retain agricultural waste (Dinar and Jammalamadaka 2013), that contribute to the maintenance and sustainable of use of the land.

The use of one service or resource can affect the level of provision of other services or resources, in a way that the severity of the appropriation problem (Botelho et al. 2013) may be reduced by the subsequent presence of these provision activities (positive externality?).

Extensive empirical research conducted in the last few decades (Hardin 1968; Feeny et al. 1990; Berkes et al. 1989) has challenged the tragic and inexorable destiny of CPRs and has built large consensus on the importance of the role of governance in CPR management.

Multiple and diverse possible responses to the fatal prediction of irreparable depletion and overharvesting of CPRs have been proposed by scholars; some referred to private property as the most efficient form of ownership (Bromley 1991; Engels 2010). In this case the resource ownership changes from common to private, and its access from free to exclusive use of the private owner and rival. This transformation should guarantee its sustainable use. Others (Schlager and Ostrom 1992) recommended government ownership and control, assuming that the regulators act in the public interest and have the authority/ability to change and organize the institution to favor the social optimum. Finally extensive empirical research conducted in the last few decades (Ostrom 1999; Olsson et al. 2004) has built large consensus on successful practices of local self-organization. According to Tacconi (2007) there are ways of transferring control over resources to communities under the framework of locally based resource management, like co-management, joint forest management, common-pool resource-based management, private access or property rights. The success of those different schemes relies on the presence of minimum environmental standards against deforestation.

None of these regimes is superior to the other; rather the best choice depends on the intrinsic features of the resource and the users. For example, empirical studies on self-organization of the communities living around a CPR, have agreed on the attributes of CPRs and of their users that enhance the probability of sustainable use. Empirical studies should aim at understanding the complex interactions between variables in particular settings, the dynamics of the systems in support of theoretical research, and policy-making.

It might be of interest to briefly discuss the concepts of government and (new) governance (Knill and Lehmkuhl 2002; Zielonka 2007; Van Kersbergen and Van Waarden 2004), with the purpose of explaining why here we refer to the latter rather than to the former, while leaving the discussion open to other political scientific research to define how the two concepts oppose or complement each other. Governing is what governments do, controlling the allocation of resources between social actors; providing rules and operating a set of institutions establishing "who gets what, where, when, and how" in society. Included in this framework is governance, which is a multi-dimensional concept that includes the activities of "establishing, promoting and supporting a specific type of relationship between governmental and non-governmental actors" (Howlett et al. 2009: 385), which are fully part of the overall governing process.

An example on how public interest and (multi-level or polycentric) governance are linked is represented by the Dutch water boards. Around 55 per cent of the area of the Netherlands is below sea level and about two-thirds of the country is vulnerable to flooding. Dutch water boards are regional government bodies, some of them having been founded in the thirteenth century, charged with managing water barriers, waterways, water levels and water quality in their respective regions. These regional water authorities, which, in collaboration in a multi-level governance with national institutions (Kaijser 2002), contribute to the national priority of controlling the risk of flooding in the Netherlands, represent the final phase of the evolution of successful multi-level governance. The history of these local authorities dates from around 800 AD, when the population pressure of the area of North Holland increased with the diffusion of new technological know-how and financial instruments. It was during this time that water control measures improved from casual non-organized interventions to structural cooperation activities within the local community. Farmers whose lands bordered directly on the dikes agreed to commit themselves to construction work and to maintenance activities, at the same time pursuing the general interest of country safety in keeping the low-lying parts dry for habitation and agriculture.

Management of forests resources

Forest resources are an example of CPRs to which different governance regimes can be applied depending on the characteristics of the forest and its users. Products and services supplied by forest resources come in two major groups. On one hand forests provide a variety of goods and services used by the local community living in the area, like wood and food production, land conservation, and water services. On the other hand there are also different types of goods and services, whose benefits affect the global community, such as carbon sink and biodiversity conservation. The approach to sustainable forest management should therefore be twofold: decentralization and self-governance by local communities with respect to the first type of services, regulation via international global agreements with respect to the second type. This distinction could be an important foundation for more effective public policies in the future.

Some authors agree that local actions and international global agreements on the management of forest resources complement each other in the final goal of sustainable resource use. According to (Ostrom and Janssen 2004: 255), "hot debates about opposites – small-scale versus large-scale, centralized versus decentralized, top-down versus bottom-up – lead nowhere."

Local governance

A large body of literature on common-pool resources (Stavins 2010) agrees on the importance of the particular values and uses of such resources that may enhance the probability that self-organization will occur (Ostrom et al. 1999; Lindberg et al. 2010). According to this categorization forests provide ecological, economic, socio-cultural, scenic and landscape services and values.

A local forest governance or a self-governed forest resource is one where actors who are the major users of the forest are involved over time in making and adapting rules in a cooperative collective choice framework regarding inclusion/exclusion of participants, appropriation strategies, obligations of participants, monitoring and sanctioning, and conflict resolution.

Issues on local forest governance are often related to some intrinsic features of the resource itself and its associated uses: the proximity of the local community to the resources, the shared values, the importance of local monitoring and shared enforcement rules, the positive effect of the voluntary provision of services of common interest by the resource appropriators. The discussion about local governance schemes is of particular interest in developing countries, generally featured by high presence of natural capital, high rate of poverty and dependence on natural resources, and often weak local governance institutions whose interests contrast with those of state authorities. According to Pulhin and Dressler (2009), community-based forest management in the Philippines is constrained by political motives and interests that adversely affect local uses of timber and local interests. In this context Tacconi's (2007) analysis of the literature on decentralized forest management leads to the conclusion that the "ideal" model of democratic decentralization of forest management in tropical forests is unlikely to be implemented due to current governance constraints and that complementary policy issues related to the implementation of decentralization programs need to be considered.

Global governance

At the international global level, growing importance has been given to the global function of forests. The recognized global benefits from a sustainable use of forests are, among others, the slowing down of deforestation, together with an increase in forestation and other management measures to improve forest areas and ecosystem productivity and biodiversity conservation, carbon emissions sequestration and contribution to slowdown of global warming (Yude Pan et al. 2011), soil protection and avoidance of soil erosion, together with weather mitigation and reduction of catastrophic weather events. In 1978 China launched the Three-North Shelterbelt Forest Program as an anti-desertification effort, which consists of forestation in northwest, north, and northeast China. The latest State Forestry Administration (SFA) data show that forest coverage in the treated areas had increased from 5.05 per cent in 1977 to 12.4 per cent at the end of 2012 (Global Times 2013).

The wide range in services of forests highlights the diversity of forest "uses," and reinforces the idea that, for many people, forests have more than the economic value currently attributed to timber production. While a lively field of literature aims at estimating the "real" value of forest resources (Pearce 1996; Chiabai et al. 2011; Lindhjem and Mitani 2012), by including in the calculation all types of goods and services, in this discussion the focus is on showing examples of global governance initiatives aimed at recognizing global forest values.

REDD+

The idea of recognizing global forest values is at the basis of REDD+ (Reducing Emissions from Deforestation and Forest Degradation, plus Conservation, sustainable management of forests and enhancement of forest carbon stocks), an international mechanism aimed at compensating developing countries that choose to reduce their carbon emissions caused by deforestation. According to this mechanism the CO_2 sequestrated in the trees owns an economic value on the international carbon markets created under the Kyoto Protocol, where tons of CO_2 are traded. Thus the forest has an economic value in not being harvested and for keeping the sequestered CO_2. Recent discussions on REDD+ have raised optimism about reducing carbon emissions and deforestation in tropical countries. If approved under the United Nations Framework Convention on Climate Change (UNFCCC), REDD+ mechanisms may generate a substantial inflow of financial resources to developing countries.

Table 8.1 Flow of transacted volumes by offset supplier and buyer region, OTC 2012

	North America	Latin America	Asia	Oceania	Europe
North America	20.3 M	–	–	–	1.2 M
Latin America	1.1 M	0.2 M	0.3 M	1.5 M	2.8 M
Africa	0.7 M	–	–	0.03 M	3.9 M
Asia	2.5 M	–	1.3 M	1 M	21.5 M
Oceania	0.3 M	–	–	1.8 M	1.7 M
Europe	1.5 M	–	–	–	0.4 M

Source: Author's elaboration on Diaz et al. (2013).

The recent report by Diaz et al. (2011) assesses the role of projects that reduce emissions from deforestation and forest degradation in 2012 compared to other sources of CO_2 emissions reduction. According to the report, 32 per cent of the transacted volumes of carbon offsets comes from forest and other land use projects, second only to RES offset projects – mainly projects for wind energy production – that represent 34 per cent of the share in the voluntary market exchange OTC. Offsets from household device and landfill methane projects represent 18 per cent of the share, while the other categories of projects – energy efficiency and fuel switch, gases, and other projects – represent in total 14.4 per cent of the traded volumes of CO_2.

Table 8.1 shows transacted volumes by offset supplier and buyer region in the international carbon market of voluntary exchange in 2012. The major offset supplier regions, Asia and Latin America, supplied Europe, North America, and Oceania with respectively 24.3, 3.6, and 2.5 million of tons of carbon offsets credits. Also Africa represents the second major offsets credits supplier of neighboring Europe, with 3.9 million of tons of CO_2 in 2012.

North America provided the second-largest source of both supply and demand in the market, with North American buyers being the primary source of demand for credits from North American projects.

Forest certification

According to some authors, forest certification (eco-labeling) is likely to make up for certain omissions in the current global forest regime (Gulbrandsen 2004; Cashore et al. 2003). Creating markets for eco-labeling would reinforce this practice. Governments do contribute, through public procurement policies and support, to creating markets

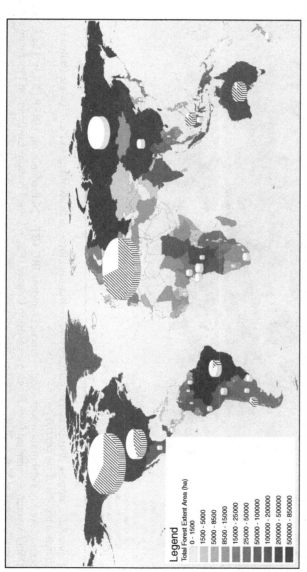

Figure 8.1 Global distribution of certified forests over total forest area according to PEFC (white section of pie charts) and FSC (hatched section of pie charts)

Source: Author's elaboration with Andrei Bocin Dumitriu JRC IET – Netherlands on UNEP (2013): The UNEP Environmental Data Explorer, as compiled from Forest Stewardship Council (FSC). United Nations Environment Programme. http://geodata.grid. unep.ch, accessed May 8, 2014.

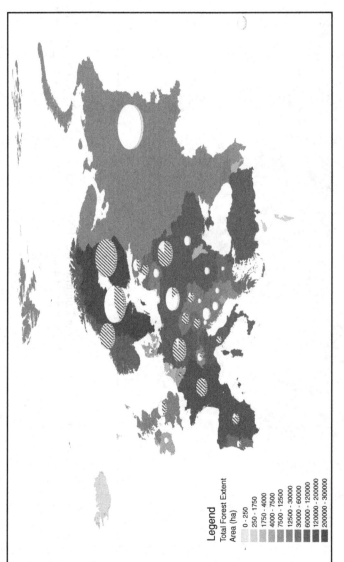

Figure 8.2 European distribution of certified forests over total forest area according to PEFC (white section of pie charts) and FSC (hatched section of pie charts)

Source: Author's elaboration with Andrei Bocin Dumitriu JRC IET – Netherlands on UNEP (2013): The UNEP Environmental Data Explorer, as compiled from Forest Stewardship Council (FSC). United Nations Environment Programme. http://geodata.grid. unep.ch, accessed May 8, 2014.

for forestry and fishery eco-labeling in many countries. Although some governments have been more skeptical, they have come to accept it as a helpful supplement to public rules and regulations (Gulbrandsen 2006).

Figures 8.1 and 8.2 represent the extent of world certified forests compared to the land covered by forest area as defined by UNEP (2010).[1] Figure 3 shows a detail of forest certification in Europe and neighboring countries.

Data used in the figure refer to two major certification organizations, the Programme for the Endorsement of Forest Certification (PEFC[2]), marked with cross-hatching on the map, and the Forest Stewardship Council (FSC[3]), marked in white.

Many other certification authorities that are not displayed in the maps operate at national level, for example Certification in Canada, the forest product association of Canada. According to the official statistics, Canada certified area at 2012 figures comprises 147,928,855 hectares certified by three different authorities: the Canadian Standards Association (CAN CSA/Z809 or Z804), the Forest Stewardship Council (FSC), and the Sustainable Forestry Initiative (SFI).

Reconciling local with global needs

A recent study by Mustalahti et al. (2012) seeks to understand how local priorities, needs, and constraints could be met through the implementation of REDD+ or forest timber certification, as they pursue the common interest of forest conservation and sustainable use. According to the study, the implementation of some forest resources projects in Tanzania under REDD+ can contribute to meeting multiple needs of the local community, such as water availability, rural development benefits, and food security.

There exists the need to reconcile local priorities and needs with global mitigation benefits, and to harmonize global and national actions with the realities of communal land and forest tenure under local governance. Discussions implementing this idea already exist. One of them is based on a national level carbon fund that would be the recipient of financial flows for avoided deforestation, carbon credit sales, and so on. In Tanzania, for instance, a fund-based approach has been argued to satisfy those needs (Burgess et al. 2013) by rewarding communities for improved forest management activities, improved forest condition, and reduced deforestation (TFWG 2010). The Kyoto Protocol provides some mechanisms that resemble REDD+ in terms of its governance structure, scale of operation, and their shared goal of contributing to local sustainable development, like the Clean

Development Mechanism. Some authors claim that the outcomes of these projects depend on the degree of community inclusion in the decision-making process, and the ability of projects to address local capacity-building needs.

The importance of interdisciplinary research and methodology

In the last 30 or 40 years anthropologists, economists, game theoreticians, historians, and political scientists have contributed to the fight against the tragedy of overuse and destruction of common resources. One might argue that indeed the solution comes from an interdisciplinary approach.

Lessons learned from the numerous empirical studies are not able to provide general conclusions, however. For this reason the governance of forest resources still lacks fundamental theories and solid hypotheses. A considerable body of theory, starting with the work of Olson (1965) and the cooperative and non-cooperative game theory, suggests important instruments for natural resources scholars in their attempt to develop a fundamental theory.

Recent studies of local resource management examine the importance of local enforcement of rules for effective resource management (Gibson et al. 2005). Various authors argue that organized monitoring of compliance of rules and sanctioning of non-conforming practices is a necessary condition for successful resource management.

> The clear prediction from a considerable body of theory, starting with the work of Mancur Olson (1965) and extended by work using non-cooperative game theory, is that no one should make any effort to refrain from harvesting from an unprotected forest in the first place. Nor should anyone be expected to engage in monitoring and rule enforcement unless they are paid to do so (and monitored by their supervisors as to how well they do their work). Voluntary provision of monitoring and sanctioning is clearly a second-order, free-rider problem.
>
> (Gibson et al. 2005: 275)

Recent work employing behavioral and experimental economics and computer simulations provides compelling evidence that not only do subjects voluntarily contribute to monitoring and sanctioning others who are non-cooperative in collective-action settings, but that rule enforcement is necessary to maintain cooperation.

Research on effective public involvement in decision-making has been conducted with the aim of reducing conflicts among multiple stakeholders of the same community and government over the use and management of forest resources. Various participatory tools such as public consultation forums and opinion polls are used to consult and to obtain inputs from communities. Involving the public in forest management decisions leads to resolving conflicts and to better management of forest resources. Multi-attribute value theory (MAVT), grounded in von Neumann and Morgenstern's utility theory, assumes the existence of a value function, based on utility maximization, to quantify public preferences in non-monetary terms. This methodology has been used to solicit and analyze stakeholder values in regional forest planning in North East Victoria, Australia (Ananda and Herath 2003).

Another technique increasingly used in a broad range of social sciences is the agent-based model approach that duplicates the actions and interactions of autonomous agents (both individual and collective entities such as organizations or groups) with a view to assessing their effects on the system as a whole. This technique has been use to analyze the pattern of land use changes and forest degradation sources (Robinson et al. 2007).

Empirical studies play a fundamental role in creating a database of information for scholars of different fields of study, as well as policy-makers and the public. Access to scientific results and exchange of information is at the core of both these principles.

Conclusion

The study of forest resource management and level of governance represents a unique opportunity for scholars from diverse fields. The complexity of the study of this topic is due to the interdisciplinary nature of the subject together with the multiple levels of stakeholders sharing the (local and global) interests in the forest resource. Research on this field is conducted at both empirical and theoretical level with the aim at reaching general understanding of the phenomenon. A quite new approach to the study of forest governance is the attempt to reconcile global, national, and local forest costs and benefits, through financial incentives rewarding the multiple social, economic, and environmental services provided by forest resources.

Notes

1 Proportion of land area covered by forest: land spanning more than 0.5 hectares with trees higher than 5 meters and a canopy cover of more than 10 per cent, or trees able to reach these thresholds *in situ*. It does not include

land that is predominantly under agricultural or urban land use. Explanatory notes: 1. Forest is determined both by the presence of trees and the absence of other predominant land uses. The trees should be able to reach a minimum height of 5 meters *in situ*. Areas under reforestation that have not yet reached but are expected to reach a canopy cover of 10 per cent and a tree height of 5 meters are included, as are temporarily unstocked areas, resulting from human intervention or natural causes, which are expected to regenerate. 2. Includes areas with bamboo and palms provided that height and canopy cover criteria are met. 3. Includes forest roads, firebreaks, and other small open areas; forest in national parks, nature reserves and other protected areas such as those of specific scientific, historical, cultural, or spiritual interest. 4. Includes windbreaks, shelterbelts, and corridors of trees with an area of more than 0.5 ha and width of more than 20 meters. 5. Includes plantations primarily used for forestry or protection purposes, such as rubber wood plantations and cork oak stands. 6. Excludes tree stands in agricultural production systems, for example in fruit plantations and agroforestry systems. The term also excludes trees in urban parks and gardens. The term is mainly related to FRA 2005 National Reporting Table T1.

2 PEFC's Chain of Custody certification is a mechanism for tracking certified material from the forest to the final product to ensure that the wood, wood fibre, or non-wood forest produce contained in the product or product line can be traced back to certified forests. It is an essential part of the PEFC system which enables companies to identify their PEFC materials. It is used to certify entities all along the value-chain of forest-based products.

3 FSC-endorsed certification of a forest site signifies that an independent evaluation by one of several FSC accredited certification bodies has shown that its management meets the internationally recognized FSC Principles and Criteria of Forest Stewardship.

References

Agarwal, C. and Singh, K. 1992. 'The Kangra Forest Co-operative Societies in Himachal Pradesh: A Case Study'. Symposium on management of rural co-operatives, Institute of Rural Management, Anand, India, 7–11 December.

Ananda, J. and Herath, G. 2003. 'Incorporating Stakeholder Values into Regional Forest Planning: A Value Function Approach'. *Ecological Economics*, 45: 75–90.

Berkes, F., Feeny, D., McCay, B. J., and Acheson, J. M. 1989. 'The Benefits of the Commons'. *Nature*, 340: 91–3.

Botelho, A., Dinar, A., Pinto, L., and Rapoport, A. 2013. 'Linking Appropriation of Common Resources and Provision of Public Goods Decreases Rate of Destruction of the Commons'. Working Paper 50. Fundacao para a ciencia y a tecnologia.

Bromley, D. W. 1991. *Environment and Economy: Property Rights and Public Policy*. Oxford: Blackwell.

Burgess, N. D., Mwakalila, S., Munishi, P. et al. 2013. 'REDD Herrings or REDD Menace: Response to Beymer-Farris and Bassett'. *Global Environmental Change*, 23: 1349–54.

Cashore, B., Auld, G., and Newsom, D. 2003. 'Forest Certification (Eco-Labeling) Programs and their Policy-Making Authority: Explaining Divergence among North American and European Case Studies'. *Forest Policy and Economics*, 5: 225–47.

Chiabai, C., Travisi, C., Markandya, A., Ding, H., and Nunes, P. 2011. 'Economic Assessment of Forest Ecosystem Services Losses: Cost of Policy Inaction'. *Environmental and Resource Economics*, 50: 405–45.

Chomitz, K. M., Buys, P., De Luca, G., Thomas, T., and Wertz-Kanounnikoff, S. 2006. *At Loggerheads? Agricultural Expansion, Poverty Reduction and Environment in the Tropical Forests*. Washington, DC: World Bank Policy Research, Development Research Group.

Diaz, D., Hamilton, K., and Johnson, E. 2011. *State of Forest Carbon Market 2011: From Canopy to Currency*. Washington, DC: Ecosystem Marketplace.

Dinar, A. and Jammalamadaka, U. K. 2013. 'Adaptation of Irrigated Agriculture to Adversity and Variability under Conditions of Drought and Likely Climate Change: Interaction between Water Institutions and Social Norms'. *International Journal of Water Governance*, 1: 41–64.

Engels, F. 2010. *The Origin of the Family, Private Property and the State*. Harmondsworth: Penguin.

Feeny, D., Berkes, F., McCay, B., and Acheson, J. 1990. 'The Tragedy of the Commons: Twenty-Two Years Later'. *Human Ecology*, 18: 1–19.

Gardner, R., Walker J., and Ostrom, E. 1990. 'Rent Dissipation in a Limited-Access Common-Pool Resource: Experimental Evidence'. *Journal of Environmental Economics and Management*, 19: 203–11.

Gibson, C. C., Williams, J., and Ostrom, E. 2005. 'Local Enforcement and Better Forests'. *World Development*, 33: 273–84.

Global Times. 2013. http://www.globaltimes.cn/content/814109.shtm, accessed May 8, 2014.

Gulbrandsen L. H. 2004. 'Overlapping Public and Private Governance: Can Forest Certification Fill the Gaps in the Global Forest Regime?' *Global Environmental Politics*, 4: 75–99.

Gulbrandsen L. H. 2006. 'Creating Markets for Eco-Labeling: Are Consumers Insignificant?' *International Journal of Consumer Studies*, 30: 477–89.

Hardin, G. 1968. 'The Tragedy of the Commons'. *Science*, 162: 1243–8.

Howlett, M., Rayner, J., and Tollefson, C. 2009. 'From Government to Governance in Forest Planning: Lessons from the Case of the British Columbia Great Bear Rainforest Initiative'. *Forest Policy and Economics*, 11: 383–91.

Kaijser, A. 2002. 'System Building from Below: Institutional Change in Dutch Water Control Systems'. *Technology and Culture*, 43: 521–48.

Knill, C. and Lehmkuhl, D. 2002. 'Private Actors and the State: Internationalization and Changing Patterns of Governance'. *Governance*, 5: 41–63.

Lindberg, K., Furze, B., Staff, M., and Black, R. 2010. *Asia-Pacific Forestry Sector Outlook Study: Ecotourism and other Services Derived From Forests in*

the Asia-Pacific Region: Outlook to 2010. Rome: Forestry Policy and Planning Division, FAO.

Lindhjem, H. and Mitani, Y. 2012. 'Forest Owners' Willingness to Accept Compensation for Voluntary Conservation: A Contingent Valuation Approach'. *Journal of Forest Economics*, 18: 290–302.

Mustalahti, I., Bolin, A., Boyd, E., and Paavola, J. 2012. 'Can REDD+ Reconcile Local Priorities and Needs with Global Mitigation Benefits? Lessons from Angai Forest, Tanzania'. *Ecology and Society*, 17: Article 16.

Olson, M. 1965. *The Logic of Collective Action: Public Goods and the Theory of Groups.* Cambridge, MA: Harvard University Press.

Olsson, P., Folke, C., and Berkes, F. 2004. 'Adaptive Co-Management for Building Resilience in Social–Ecological Systems'. *Environmental Management*, 34: 75–90.

Ostrom E. 1999. *Self-Governance and Forest Resources.* Bogor, Indonesia: CIFOR.

Ostrom, E., Burger, J., Field, C., Norgaard, R., and Policansky, D. 1999. 'Revisiting the Commons: Local Lessons, Global Challenges'. *Science*, 284: 278–82.

Ostrom E. and Janssen, M. 2004. 'Multilevel Governance and Resilience of Social-Ecological Systems', in M. Spoor (ed.), *Globalization, Poverty and Conflict.* Dordrecht: Kluwer, pp. 239–60.

Pearce, D. 1996. 'Global Environmental Value and the Tropical Forests: Demonstration and Capture', in W. Adamowicz, P. Boxall, M. Luckett, W. Phillips, and W. White (eds.), *Forestry, Economics and the Environment.* Wallingford: CAB International, pp. 11–48.

Pulhin, J. and Dressler, W. 2009. 'People, Power and Timber: The Politics of Community-Based Forest Management'. *Journal of Environmental Management*, 91: 206–14.

Robinson, T., Brown, D., Parker, D. et al. 2007. 'Comparison of Empirical Methods for Building Agent-Based Models in Land Use Science'. *Journal of Land Use Science*, 2: 31–55.

Schlager, E. and Ostrom, E. 1992. 'Property-Rights Regimes and Natural Resources: A Conceptual Analysis'. *Land Economics*, 68: 249–62.

Stavins, R. 2010. 'The Problem of the Commons: Still Unsettled after 100 Years'. FEEM Nota di Lavoro 131.

Tacconi, L. 2007. 'Decentralization, Forests and Livelihoods: Theory and Narrative'. *Global Environmental Change*, 17: 338–48.

Tanzania Forestry Working Group (TFWG). 2010. 'Options for REDD in Tanzania: Key Design Issues for the National REDD Strategy'. Brief 2, September. http://www.tfcg.org/pdf/Brief%202%20Key%20Design%20Issues%20for%20REDD%20Strategy.pdf, accessed May 8, 2014.

UNEP. 2010. *The UNEP Environmental Data Explorer, as compiled from Forest Stewardship Council (FSC).* Tratto da United Nations Environment Programme: http://geodata.grid.unep.ch, accessed May 8, 2014.

Van Kersbergen, K. and Van Waarden, F. 2004. '"Governance" as a Bridge between Disciplines: Cross-Disciplinary Inspiration Regarding Shifts in

Governance and Problems of Governability, Accountability and Legitimacy'. *European Journal of Political Research*, 43: 143–71.

Yude Pan, Birdsey, R., Fang, J. et al. 2011. 'A Large and Persistent Carbon Sink in the World's Forests'. *Science*, 333: 988–93.

Zielonka, J. 2007. 'Plurilateral Governance in the Enlarged European Union'. *Journal of Common Market Studies*, 45: 187–209.

Index

Printed in the United States
by Baker & Taylor Publisher Services